LEITH SANDS

CHARACTERS

In order of appearance

RAB SOUTER.
BELLE HEPBURN.
DUNCAN FORBES.
ALEXANDER LOCKHART.
WILL GOW.

JOHN MASSON.
JAMES KERR.
PETER BEATTIE.
SANDY CRAIG.

A taproom in Leith, on the 11th of April 1705. In the back wall are two deep-set windows giving on the street, and, left of them, the door, now closed. Against the right wall, behind a rough counter, is the stock-in-trade : claret and brandy, a cask of ale, and whisky. A bench and long table below the windows, another by the left wall, and a smaller table with wooden chairs nearer the middle of the room.

The wind that is rarely still on that windy coast blows against the windows in long gusts, but it is snug enough in the room, which is clean and well kept, as if the owner took a pride in it.

The proprietor, RAB SOUTER, is pouring a drink behind the bar. He is small, middle-aged, canny, honest, and self-respecting. Not the type to lead a crusade ; but the kind of man who likes to " see right done " and is vaguely troubled at the vivid prejudices of his fellow-men. He is alone except for one customer, BELLE HEPBURN, who is sitting with her back to the nearer window. BELLE is not yet old enough for her profession to have ruined her looks, but the mixture of vanity and greed that led to her adoption of her calling ruins effectually enough any beauty she possesses. Her face, for all its excellence of feature and colouring, is a repellent one.

RAB. [*Carrying the drink to her and putting it down*] There you are. I hope you've the money to pay for it.

BELLE. [*Taking out money*] It'll be a while yet before I lack the

7

price of a drink, Rab Souter. [*Toasting him*] Well! [*Having drunk*] I didn't think you'd be open. Why are you no' at the hanging? Half Scotland's there.

RAB. Maybe. But trade's trade.

BELLE. And some has weak stomachs.

RAB. [*Stung, but still mildly*] If it comes to that, why are you not there yersel? It's thanks to you they're hanging, isn't it?

BELLE. [*Screaming at him*] Haud yer tongue! [*Recovering*] I was there, if you want to know. There was sic a crowd I couldn't see a thing, so I just came away.

RAB. [*Pausing in the polishing of mugs at the counter*] Confess, Belle Hepburn, you didn't after all want to see a man you'd slept with dangling at the end of a rope.

BELLE. Is it me would care that a wheen stuck-up Englishmen went to their deaths?

RAB. He was a well set up young fellow, Captain Green. I saw him one day coming from the trial.

BELLE. [*Without emotion*] Ay, he was bonnie enough. [*With satisfaction*] But he was a pirate, and he's hanging for it.

RAB. There's some say he's hanging because he's English.

BELLE. [*Banging her mug-bottom against the table in anger*] So! A " repriever ", are you!

RAB. [*Hastily*] I'm not anything. I'm just repeating the clash of the town.

BELLE. Well, don't repeat a thing like that if you like your health. *And* your trade! This place would make a fine bonfire.

RAB. [*Rousing to a threat of coercion as he has not roused to her taunt of being weak-stomached*] Things are coming to a pretty pass when a man can't open his mouth without fear of being rabbled.

BELLE. You can open it, but not so wide.

RAB. And when the likes of you gives orders to the likes of me! Let me tell you, I don't like Englishmen any better than the next Scot, but there's one thing in this business sticks in my gullet.

BELLE. It wouldn't be your tongue, would it?

RAB. If he's a pirate, why wasn't there a single thing in his ship that didn't belong there? [*He says this not as one making a point but as one troubled by an undeniable fact.*]

BELLE. He had Sandy Craig's watch, hadn't he?

8

LEITH SANDS

LEITH SANDS

AND OTHER SHORT PLAYS

BY
GORDON DAVIOT

DUCKWORTH
HENRIETTA STREET, LONDON, W.C.

First Published 1946

PRINTED IN GREAT BRITAIN BY
MORRISON AND GIBB LTD., LONDON AND EDINBURGH

CONTENTS

RAB. So *you* say.

BELLE. And what's wrong with my word!

RAB. Nothing. Only, where's the watch?

BELLE. It was stolen from him, he said. Likely he threw it away. [*Protesting against* RAB'S *unbelieving silence*] I tell you he had that watch the day he came ashore! Didn't I go out to the *Worcester* when she anchored? And didn't he come back with me when he got rid of all the yapping big-wigs that wanted to see the ship? [*Imitating polite Edinburgh*] " And have you really been to India and back, Captain Green? " " How clever of you to escape the French by sailing round Scotland to London, Captain Green! " And next morning, there was the watch, lying on my table. " Where did you get that? " says I. " It was my father's," says he. But it was Sandy Craig's watch, with the anchor on the back of it. Many a time I'd seen it before. And Sandy Craig went away in the *Speedy Return* last year. And who has seen the *Speedy Return*, or any of her crew, since that day?

RAB. [*Slowly*] An anchor's not a mighty uncommon thing to find on a sailor's belongings. Even if you did see the watch——

BELLE. [*Furious*] Even if I did see it! What would I lie for?

RAB. [*Still contemplative*] How should I know? Because you don't like Englishmen, perhaps; or because you wanted one of his Indian shawls and he wouldn't give it to you; or because he took up with a nice self-respecting girl and forgot you; or because someone offered you good silver to remember seeing the watch——

BELLE. Are you suggesting . . .

RAB. I'm not suggesting anything. I'm only thinking of things that would make a woman want to tell lies.

BELLE. Let me tell you . . .

> *She pauses, as* RAB'S *eyes watch someone pass the windows, and turns her head to the door to see who comes.*
>
> *Enter* DUNCAN FORBES. *He is very young; a law student of twenty; and he is dressed entirely in black. He has a long shrewd nose which augurs well for his future success in his profession, and a wide good-natured*

*mouth to promise humanity in his shrewdest dealings.
At the moment his normally mobile face is wooden;
stiff with some secret shock or grief. He moves forward
to the counter without acknowledging the landlord's
presence, as if his mind was still elsewhere.*

RAB. [*Greeting him*] Good day to you, Mr. Forbes, sir. The usual for you?

FORBES. No. Give me whisky.

RAB. [*Thinking he could not have heard aright*] I still have some of that last bordeaux that you liked so much . . .

FORBES. [*Unmistakably*] Whisky!

RAB. [*Pouring the required drink, genially*] In all the times you've been coming down for your daunder on Leith sands, Mr. Forbes, I've never known you drink that stuff. Do you want to lose that fine palate of yours?

FORBES. [*After a slight pause, as if talking were an effort*] No. I want to lose my senses.

RAB. [*Having considered him, tentatively*] Are you in mourning, sir?

FORBES. Yes. For my country. [*Without heat*] If I could burn the Scot out of me with hot iron I would do it to-day. It's a dreadful thing to be ashamed of the very blood in one's veins, isn't it, Rab? [*Pushes his empty glass to be refilled.*]

BELLE. [*Into the silence while* RAB *is looking for an answer*] If that's the way you feel it's time someone let a little of your blood out, my fine young sir!

FORBES. [*Becoming aware of her for the first time, and turning to look at her; in slow recognition*] Oh. The Hepburn woman. [*He does not mean to be rude. He is still wrapt in himself.*]

BELLE. Mistress Hepburn to you.

FORBES. Well, I suppose drink is as good a way as any other of spending thirty pieces.

BELLE. I don't know what that may mean, but it has a quarrelling sound to me.

FORBES. Thomas Green was looking forward to drinking too. In peace, in a London tavern. All his dangers were behind him. The storms off the Cape, the pirates in the Indian Ocean, the French in the Channel; fever and snake-bite and thirst-madness and mirage. He had traded well, and his cargo was rich. He had taken his ship half round the world and back like a good seaman ; and he was a proud young man sailing into the Forth ; home again and safe. No one had told him that Scotland was still inhabited by savages.

> *He turns to the counter again and takes the drink that* RAB *has poured for him.*
>
> *As he turns to his drink the door is burst open and three men enter, all in jovial spirits and talking as they come. The first is* ALEXANDER LOCKHART, *well-built, about forty years old, "well put on" and tolerably well educated ; belonging, one would say, to the small-official class. Behind him is* WILL GOW, *tall, lean, saturnine ; perhaps a printer or a clerk. And bringing up the rear* JOHN MASSON, *a small, thickset, genial creature, whose thicker burr and slight air of deference place him in a lower social category.*
>
> *They arrange themselves in the chairs round the small table as they talk, with much clatter and no little self-satisfaction.*

LOCKHART. [*As he comes in*] And it's my suggestion that April the Eleventh should be made a national holiday for ever.

GOW. [*Grinning*] The Kirk wouldn't like it.

MASSON. [*With a fling at the thousand schisms of Scotland*] Which kirk ?

GOW. All of them. Holidays are a devilish rival to the Sabbath.

LOCKHART. Maybe ; but there isn't a minister in Scotland who didn't lose his spare silver in the Darien scheme. Brandy for me, Rab.

MASSON. Ay ; that's so. Not that it needed Darien. Our man [*he means his own particular clergyman*] 's been praying against the English since afore the Revolution. I doubt he'd look real kindly on a day that saw three of them get their deserts. [*Answering* LOCKHART'S *invitation*] Ale for me, Mr. Lockhart.

LOCKHART. Tuts, man, you're not going to drink ale on a day like this ! Brandy for Mr. Masson, Rob. What are you drinking, Gow ?

GOW. Claret for me. Ah, there, Belle !

LOCKHART. [*Turning to the woman*] Good day to you, Mistress

Hepburn. A good day indeed, eh ? Drink up and have another one with us. [*It is clear that in normal times* LOCKHART *would not have " looked the road she was on ", but to-day all Scots are brothers together, and has she not done her share in the noble work ?*] Were you out there on the sands ?

BELLE. [*Without bothering to explain that she had left betimes*] I was. [*Directing the remark at* FORBES' *back*] Ay, a good day for Scotland.

> *The door is once more burst open and there enters* JAMES
> KERR, *a man who might be a prosperous small-trades-
> man, more or less supporting the large and undoubtedly
> drunk person of* PETER BEATTIE. BEATTIE *can still
> walk with comparative ease, but his head has long ago
> succumbed to the drunkard's* idée fixe.

KERR. There we are, Peter boy. Home from home. [*He bangs the door to behind him and unfastens the short sword that is belted to his waist*] Well, I won't be needing *this* any more. [*Flinging it on the long table, left*] Three months that thing's been tripping me up. Next time we have to arm I'll get me a cudgel. [*Like the rest, he is in very good humour about it.*]

BEATTIE. [*Standing aimless and stupid by the table*] Down with England ! Down with Englishmen ! Scotland for ever ! [*After a moment he subsides on to the bench by the left wall.*]

> GOW, *reminded of his own weapons, takes his heavy pistol
> from a pocket and lays it on the table in front of him,
> while* MASSON *unbuckles a truncheon from below his
> coat.* LOCKHART *continues to wear his sword, which he
> considers helpful in presenting a gentlemanly appearance.*

GOW. [*Picking up the pistol fondly almost as soon as he has put it down*] The muzzle of that was three inches from the Chancellor's nose in the High Street yesterday. Talk of reprieve, would they !

LOCKHART. They've learned their lesson.

GOW. " The Queen is considering the evidence, and will let her decision be known in due course " ! [*He laughs*] Well, she has evidence now that the Scots can decide for themselves.

KERR. [*As* RAB *puts the brandy down in front of* LOCKHART] Bring me some of that, Mr. Souter. [*Giving* BEATTIE *a friendly push*] Rouse yourself, Peter Beattie, and say what you'll drink.

BEATTIE. I'll drink Scotland dry.

KERR. Not unless you're paying for your own liquor, my mannie! [*To* RAB] Bring him the same as me. [*To the others*] Ay, gentlemen, we've struck a blow for freedom this day. We're not going to have any fine fellows in London interfering in the decisions of our courts.

MASSON. No, nor Queen Anne herself.

GOW. Reprieve a murderer, would they!

LOCKHART. [*Raising his glass*] Well, here's the same death to every Englishman that thinks he can pirate a Scots ship and go free!

GOW. [*Joining him*] Damnation to Englishmen anyhow! [MASSON *drinks too.*]

KERR. I suppose he didn't confess, did he? I couldn't hear his speech.

LOCKHART. Confess, my friend! His speech made me want to puke. He was so innocent, by his way of it, you'd wonder how he ever came to leave his dame's-school. And the other two weren't much better.

GOW. [*Mocking*] Very affecting, it was. I'll wager Belle didn't shed any tears.

BELLE. No; I'll keep my tears for the crew of the *Speedy Return*. [*With a meaning look at* FORBES' *back*] Though there's some not so particular!

> LOCKHART *and his two companions waken to an intense interest in the man whose face they cannot see and whom they have up to now hardly been aware of.* BELLE, *her eyes discreetly on her drink, waits developments with inward pleasure.*

KERR. [*Unaware of the direction of her last remark, and not having met her before*] Mistress Hepburn, is it? Well, well. I'm proud to know you, Mistress Hepburn. [*With unctious earnestness*] Sandy Craig will sleep well to-night, now that his countrymen have avenged him.

BEATTIE. [*Apropos of nothing, except that he now has his drink and is momentarily roused to speech*] Thieving, murdering English. Keep us out of their trade, will they? We'll show them.

KERR. Gentlemen, I give you the memory of Captain Drummond and the crew of the *Speedy Return*, foully done to death by the murderer Green.

LOCKHART. And all the other victims of his piracies, whoever they may be ! [*His eyes are still speculatively on* FORBES' *back, and his voice is provocative. Pausing before drinking*] Won't you join us, sir, in so loyal a toast ?

FORBES. [*Who has had a third drink but is still cool, turning to face him*] There was only one case of piracy in this affair, Alexander Lockhart. And that was when you and your gang boarded the *Worcester* as friendly visitors and seized her, with neither law nor good manners on your side.

LOCKHART. [*Restraining* GOW's *instant movement to his weapon*] Just a moment, Gow. I don't admire your sentiments, sir, but I wonder at your courage. You're a young man to be tired of life.

FORBES. If giving up my life would blot this day's work from my country's record, I would die gladly.

GOW. [*Still being restrained by* LOCKHART] You'll probably die in any case !

MASSON. [*Aghast*] Did ever you hear the like of his impudence !

LOCKHART. So you don't approve of your country's justice ?

FORBES. Justice !

LOCKHART. You think, no doubt, it's a crying shame that the Englishmen weren't reprieved ?

FORBES. [*With the first hint of passion in his tone*] No. I think it is a black disgrace that they were ever found guilty. [*Sensation.*] We have hanged three men to-day—and we are going to hang more to-morrow—on evidence that would not convict a cat of stealing cream. And why were they hanged ? Because Scotland wanted a blood sacrifice. Because we had failed to make colonies like the English, and failed to keep ships on the sea like the English, and we were sick with jealousy and drunk with hate and shouting for blood. Well, we have had our blood. But my business is law, not murder, and you will forgive me if I do not share in the jubilation.

KERR. [*Bewildered at the way this nice friendly drinking party is turning out*] But that's nonsense ! I was there, a whole day, at the trial ; I was there myself. There was plenty evidence !

14

MASSON. It was his own men that gave evidence against him !

LOCKHART. May I remind you that there was no mention of piracy until one of the *Worcester*'s crew boasted of it ?

FORBES. Did you ever know a sailor who wasn't a pirate after the third drink ? There was no mention of piracy, Mr. Lockhart, until *you* found that your seizing of the *Worcester* was going to be awkward for you. You thought she was an East Indiaman, didn't you ? And you would take her as reprisal for the *Annandale*——

MASSON. The English had no right to take the *Annandale*.

FORBES. They had every right. She had broken the law, and they took her by law. It is an English custom that we would do well to imitate. But Green's ship had broken no law. She was not even, so it turned out, one of the hated East Indiamen. It was going to be very awkward for those who had so rashly——

GOW. [*Who has been simmering in speechless rage, springing up*] Are you going to let him stand there and fling it in our faces that we—— [LOCKHART *once more restrains him, as* RAB *remonstrates with* FORBES.)

RAB. [*Laying a tentative hand on* FORBES' *shoulder from behind, in appeal*] Please, Mr. Forbes, sir. We don't want any trouble.

FORBES. [*His taut nerves snapping at the touch, turning on* RAB] No, you don't want trouble ! And you the guiltiest of them all. [*Seeing* RAB'S *astounded face*] Do you think Green and his men are dangling out there in the wind only because a vain drab lied and because the mob hate England ? No, they're——

BELLE. Call me a liar——!

LOCKHART. I've let you talk long enough——

FORBES. [*Shouting them down*] Hold your tongues ! [*As they stop in very astonishment*] No ! They're swinging there because the nice douce citizens of Edinburgh didn't want any trouble. Because a few innocent men hanging at their door was better than having their windows broken——

KERR. Innocent men, indeed !

MASSON. It's not windows that would be broken but heads if they'd let that murdering pirate go free.

KERR. I heard the evidence myself. Wasn't it one of his own men who told how they killed their victims with hatchets and flung them overboard. One of his own men!

FORBES. [*The excitement gone from him; in a sort of weary contempt*] Yes. A black cook's mate who understood no English, was so poor that he would have sworn to anything for a shilling, and was proved not to have joined the *Worcester* until six months after the date in question.

LOCKHART. The ship's surgeon isn't black, nor illiterate, nor poor enough to bribe with a shilling.

FORBES. No. He is a man with a grudge. In fact, he hated Green so much that I am surprised he didn't make his story a better one.

LOCKHART. His story was true.

FORBES. Perhaps. What does it amount to? He was ashore and he heard guns; he went on board some days later and three of the crew were wounded. The guns were the *Worcester*'s salute to Captain Grandell's ship and Grandell's five-gun acknowledgment; and the "wounds" prove to have been one snake bite, one broken arm through falling down a hatch, and one head broken by a bottle. Is that your evidence of piracy? And where in all this is the *Speedy Return*? Not so much as a rope's-end of her! Not even a suggestion that she was ever in the same sea with the *Worcester*!

BELLE. [*Shrilly*] No? Then how was Sandy Craig's watch in her captain's pocket?

FORBES. Was it?

BELLE. It was, and I'll thank you not to call me a liar to my face again!

FORBES. [*Taking two steps towards her so that only the table separates them, and leaning forward so that they are face to face*] Why didn't you wait to see Green hanged?

BELLE. [*Taken aback by his unexpected movement, his proximity, and his surprising question*] What's that you say?

FORBES. I said: Why didn't you wait to see Green hanged?

> *The others begin to protest that she has seen the man hanged, that she has said so; but their protests die away as* BELLE's *face shows her confusion.*

BELLE. [*Knowing that* RAB *is a witness to her early departure, and unable in the crowded moment to think what her previous excuse was*] Never mind why! What I do or don't do is my own business. [*It sounds very feeble, and the pause on* FORBES' *part before he straightens himself gives the feebleness full effect.*]

FORBES. [*Resuming as if he had not spoken to her*] Captain Green said that his watch had a cross on the back of it, and that he had never owned a watch engraved with an anchor.

BELLE. [*Sullenly*] It was an anchor, and it was Sandy Craig's.

FORBES. [*Ignoring her*] May I suggest that the two decorations look greatly alike and that it is possible to be—mistaken, shall we say?—about them.

BEATTIE. [*Quite unaware of anything that is going on around him*] Bloody murdering English, keeping us out of their trade!

FORBES. In the months that the *Worcester* has been lying at Burntisland [*he tilts his head to an imaginary firth*] industrious Scots have torn the very planks out of her in search of better evidence than an unproducible watch. And what have they found? Nothing! There wasn't a nail in her that couldn't be accounted for. No stolen goods, no bloodstains, no damage by gunfire, no false entries in her papers. [*Overriding interruption*] Seventeen ships have come home from India since the *Worcester* sailed from there, and not one of them has heard of any such piracy. [*Overriding interruption*] When the *Worcester*'s own crew first heard that they were to be charged with such a crime they were scattered in lodgings all over the district. Did any one of them try to escape? On the contrary: several came in of their own accord. It seemed to all of them amusing to be dubbed pirates, when there was no tittle of evidence to support the charge. But they reckoned without my countrymen. Fifteen good Scots found them guilty——

[*Chorus*]. They were guilty! Guilty as hell! Murdering cut-throats, whatever you say!

FORBES. Found them guilty on the evidence of a black slave who was not there, of a ship's surgeon who was on shore, and of a woman who saw an old lover's watch in the hands of a presumed murderer and made no outcry until five weeks later, when evidence of piracy was wanted.

He turns to his ready-filled glass, and so gives his inter-
rupters their chance at last. BELLE, KERR, GOW *and*
MASSON *all have things to say, but give way to* LOCKHART
after the first few words.

LOCKHART. [*Angry but smooth*] You've a fine, glib tongue, my
friend, and you may know something about law, but I'd just
remind you that no less than five of those fifteen men were
ships' masters, and perhaps you'll allow them to know something
of sea business.

FORBES. [*Turning on him*] And what sea business moves their
mariner minds at the moment? The *Annandale*! What moves
the whole of Scotland, if it comes to that? The English con-
fiscate our last Company ship in the Thames—the English, who
have fifty ships to our one!—and you think that five ships'
captains in a jury of fifteen make a good——

KERR. There were ten others, weren't there! Ten that had
nothing to do with the sea. Lairds like Fleming of Rathbyres
and merchants like William Neilson——

GOW. Ay, well-respected men like Robert Innes——

LOCKHART. Ay, do you think folk like Forrest and Blockwood
are going to vote a prisoner guilty just because a few men in
London acted unneighbourly?

FORBES. No.

LOCKHART. Why did they, then!

FORBES. I take it, because twenty thousand armed men were
waiting for them outside the court-house in Edinburgh. [*Into
the momentary pause which succeeds this riposte*] And when the
verdict was noised abroad, and the gratified Scots were dancing
in the streets, what did those same unneighbourly English do?
Did they threaten? Was there talk of war? Or promise of
reprisal if we hanged their men? No! They asked that
the day of execution might be postponed for two weeks, so
that——

MASSON. Ay, so that they could think of a way of wriggling
out!

FORBES. So that there might be time to collect more evidence.

LOCKHART. They had three months to collect evidence if
they'd wanted to.

FORBES. You forget. There was no case to answer. It would hardly occur to the English that men could be condemned on a piece of hearsay.

KERR. They were condemned because they were guilty. I heard the evidence myself!

FORBES. [*Ignoring him*] When they learned what perjury and prejudice had achieved in Scotland they wanted time to defend their men; time to use their own weapons of statement and evidence——

GOW. Time to use fresh lies——

FORBES. Time! Time! Time! That is all they asked. And every one of them from Queen Anne to the crossing-sweeper in the Strand took it for granted that we would give it to them. We were civilised, weren't we? We had courts and laws. We ate our bread and powdered our wigs like other men. We sent embassies to the nations, and shared a Queen with England. We would not hang fourteen men without making sure that they were guilty. How were they to know, the trusting English fools, that they were dealing with barbarians?

LOCKHART. If that is meant as a personal reflection . . .

FORBES. [*His natural courage no wise lessened by the consumption of his fourth drink*] It's a reflection on all of you! On all the venomous mob that refused a hearing to condemned men, so that our country's name will be a by-word in Europe. You were afraid of what that evidence from London might be, weren't you? Afraid of finding that you wouldn't be able to hang the Englishmen after all? Already some very awkward facts had blown up from the south. The surgeon had said in his evidence that the captured ship was sold in Quillon, hadn't he? And now the English send proof that no one in Quillon had ever heard of it. That was awkward, wasn't it? And every post that came into Edinburgh might carry news as awkward. It looked as if you might be cheated of the blood you had so nearly tasted——

LOCKHART. You're drunk!

FORBES. Alas, no!

GOW. Why are we listening to him? Let's cut the clattering tongue out of his head.

RAB. Please, gentlemen. Please, Mr. Forbes.

Masson. Ay, I cracked a man's skull yesterday for saying a hundredth part of what he's saying the now.

Lockhart. Presently, presently. You're not cutting out his tongue till he's taken back a few of his words.

Forbes. I'll take back nothing.

Lockhart. This is a personal matter between me and Mr. . . .

Forbes. My name is Forbes. Duncan Forbes.

Lockhart. Between me and Mr. Forbes. He can greet all he likes about his country's reputation—Scotland can take care of her own good name!—but when he miscalls a man to his face he has to answer for it. [*His left hand draws his sword a few inches from its sheath and lets it fall back again with a click.*]

Rab. Mr. Forbes is a bit overwrought, Mr. Lockhart, and the whisky he's been drinking is not good stuff to take counsel on——

Lockhart. [*Ignoring him*] I doubt too many hours in the law courts has made him forget that the law's privileges stop at the court door. Outside that a man's answerable for what he says.

Forbes. If you're thinking of using that fine sword of yours, Mr. Lockhart, I think it's only fair to tell you that I may be a law student, but I was born the wrong side of the Highland line and I was bred to the sword.

Lockhart. [*Obviously staggered, but recovering, and very angry*] Who said anything about a sword ? I wouldn't waste good steel on you, you damned Highland trash. I'll wring your neck myself when Gow's had the pleasure of cutting your tongue out.

Masson. Don't I get a share ?

Lockhart. Meanwhile, as long as your gullet's in working order, I'll give myself the pleasure of hearing you swallow some of these fine words of yours.

Belle. Ay, make him swallow what he said about me !

Lockhart. Hold your tongue. [*To* Forbes] There was something about my seizing the *Worcester* when I had no right to . . .

Forbes. And didn't you ?

Lockhart. And raising the cry of piracy merely to get myself out of a hole !

Forbes. I may have been wrong about that.

Lockhart. So !

Forbes. It may of course have been to get yourself some

the rich pickings the cargo would provide. There is no direct evidence either way.

LOCKHART. Damn your soul, do you say that I procured false witness to hang those men!

FORBES. Is that any worse than standing over the Privy Council with pistols to prevent them postponing the execution? That is what you were doing all day yesterday, wasn't it?

LOCKHART. And to-morrow I shall be explaining to your friends how you fell over an ale-house counter and broke your neck. [*He takes a step forward, and becomes aware that a small black knife has appeared as if by magic in* FORBES' *hand. He is holding it Highland fashion, point upward. He has not altered his attitude, and the knife might not be there unless one noticed his hand.*] What good do you think that bodkin's going to do you?

FORBES. It's been a lot of good so far. I've cut rodden whistles with it, and gralloched a deer with it, and cut a heart on a tree with it, and picked stones out of my pony's——

GOW. And picked your teeth with it. Go on!

The others laugh.

FORBES. And I can split a hazel wand at twenty feet with it. [*Something in his still easy tone gives them pause*] It's a pretty weapon the sword [*there is genuine love in his voice*] but I gave it up when I took to the law. It seemed to me that Scotland had suffered enough from her children's liking for steel. I could serve her better by learning how to arbitrate. But I can still throw a knife quicker than any of you gentlemen can move an arm. I hope you wont force me to display my skill. It would be sad to have renounced the sword only to become a knife-thrower.

LOCKHART. There's only one thing wrong with your bodkin, Mr. Forbes. It doesn't throw five ways at once.

FORBES. And which of you is going to be the sheath for it?

GOW. That's for you to decide. We're coming together and you can take your pick. For myself, a knife-prick will be a small price for the pleasure of having my hands on you.

LOCKHART. If you know any prayers, say them. And don't make them long ones.

21

RAB. You can't do it, gentlemen. At least give him a sword and let him fight for his——

GOW. Shut your mouth, you, or we'll make a loch of your liquor and drown you in it!

BEATTIE. Bloody Englishmen, are they? Kill them!

LOCKHART. Well, Forbes, have you prayed?

> *On a great gust of wind there enters a smallish red-haired man carrying a sailor's bundle. He bangs the door to behind him with his foot, as KERR did, and drops his bundle by the door. Since no one has yet reached for a weapon, the scene in the room appears to him perfectly normal: one man leaning against the counter and facing the others in argument. Except for head-turning no one moves at his entrance, but as he speaks BELLE, recognising him, rises slowly to her feet. He is SANDY CRAIG.*

SANDY. Whew! Blowing a half-gale as usual. Leith was aye a windy port. A fine day to come home, too. [*With a jerk of his thumb to outdoors*] Is it the Privy Council they're hanging? You could walk on the heads of the crowd halfway to Edinburgh!

BELLE. [*Still not sure whether to believe her eyes, and hoping that she is wrong*] Sandy! Sandy Craig!

SANDY. [*Noticing her for the first time; in high good humour*] Belle! Well, now, this is what I call a welcome! [*He means finding an old friend so soon.*] Belle, my beauty . . . [*He goes towards her, but she draws back.*]

BELLE. You're not dead?

SANDY. [*Mistaking her tone*] Och, have you been crying for me! [*As she shrinks from his outstretched hand*] What is it? Are you afraid I'm a ghost? [*Rapping with his knuckles on the table*] A good solid ghost, let me tell you; and one with a thirst. [*Moving to the counter*] Is nobody going to offer a sailor a drink? [*As they stare in silence*] Well [*turning in good humour to* RAB], it looks as if I'll have to pay for my own. That'll be the first time for three years. What a country to belong to!

FORBES. [*The first to come to life, quietly*] Are you Sandy Craig?

SANDY. I am. [*To* RAB] Brandy.

FORBES. Of the *Speedy Return*?

SANDY. Ay, of the *Speedy Return*. That was a bad name to call a good ship !

FORBES. What happened to her ?

SANDY. Pirates got her, eighteen months ago.

BELLE. [*Shrill with relief*] I was right, you see, I was right !

SANDY. You were always right, Belle, my dear.

BELLE. He had your watch. [*It seems to her that a miracle has happened.*]

SANDY. Who had ?

BELLE. Captain Green.

SANDY. Captain Green ? Never heard of him. What's he captain of ?

FORBES. He was [*he slightly accents the tense*] captain of the *Worcester*.

SANDY. Never heard of her. East Indiaman ?

BELLE. You mean it wasn't the *Worcester* that took the *Speedy Return* !

SANDY. It wasn't any ship at all that took us. That old pirate Bowen walked on board when she was in harbour in Madagascar, and just hung up his hat. All the crew was ashore but three, and they had more sense than to argue with Bowen. [*As the queerness in the atmosphere begins to penetrate*] What's this to do with Captain Green, anyhow ?

> *In the silence,* FORBES *drops some coins on the counter and turns to depart. The various emotions that have upheld him are spent, and he is suddenly exhausted and a little drunk. He looks so ill that* RAB *is concerned.*

RAB. Will I send for your horse, Mr. Forbes ? Are you going back to Edinburgh ?

FORBES. [*Gathering himself together with an effort*] No. No, I am going to help bury the men we have murdered.

> *They watch him go in silence. As he closes the door,* BELLE *begins to sob.*

SLOW CURTAIN

23

RAHAB

CHARACTERS

In order of appearance

RAHAB.	CARMI.
SHUAH.	A CAPTAIN.
MAHLON.	SOLDIERS.

The living-room in the house of RAHAB, *on the wall of Jericho, about the year 1451 B.C. In the back wall is the doorway, giving on to a terrace which overlooks the street a few feet below. The street one cannot see, but in the distance are flat white roofs and a piece of sky. In the right corner is a low bed piled with rugs. Down right is a small window giving on to the country outside the city walls. Down left an opening into an inner room. On the left wall a mirror, and below it a low table. Up-stage of the table two large jars, one of water and one of wine. Down from the bed a wooden chest. On the table, toilet articles and sewing materials.*

RAHAB *is lying on the bed, ankles crossed and arms behind her head, staring at the ceiling. She is a handsome woman, not in her first youth, but still beautiful and possessing the sureness that is beauty's legacy.*

Enter SHUAH, *from the inner room, folding a linen cloth. She is sixty, and looks it ; a sharp face and an unwieldy body.*

SHUAH. It has stopped raining. [RAHAB *takes no notice.*] I say : the rain has stopped.

RAHAB. [*In a rich, lazy voice*] You excite me. [*She has not moved an eyelash.*]

SHUAH. Someone must go to market or there will be nothing for supper.

RAHAB. Yes.

SHUAH. Do you want to go, or shall I ?

RAHAB. You go.

SHUAH. [*Protesting*] It is good business to show yourself in the market. It keeps people from forgetting you.

RAHAB. They are in no danger of forgetting me. Not yet.

SHUAH. You're not as young as you were, you know.

RAHAB. How dull life would be without your singing, my little mosquito.

SHUAH. When I was your age I used to invent errands, so that I could watch the heads turn. You will get too fat lying there staring at the ceiling.

RAHAB. At least my hips will not spread with sitting. [*Rolling over a little to look at* SHUAH] It annoys you, doesn't it, Shuah, to see someone doing nothing.

SHUAH. Yes, it does. It's not natural. What is there to think about ?

RAHAB. [*Rolling on to her back again*] I was thinking that a thousand years from now no one will know that we have lived. It is a horrible thought. Have you ever considered it ? No one will remember anything about us.

SHUAH. Why should you expect them to ?

RAHAB. I don't expect them to. It is because I don't that . . . [*Giving up the attempt to interpret for the unimaginative* SHUAH] Oh, well.

SHUAH. I need money if I am going to the market.

RAHAB. In the toe of my red shoe.

SHUAH. [*Going to the shoes, which are lying by the wall below the mirror*] That's a daft place.

RAHAB. A shoe is safer than a girdle when one lives on the wall.

SHUAH. [*Examining the coins*] The cavalryman wasn't over-generous. I suppose I must change my sandals if I am to go wading through the puddles. [*Changing her sandals for clog-like shoes*] The paving of this town is a disgrace. Taxes for the army, and taxes for the temple, and taxes to keep the cavalry horses in shoes, but not a thought for poor old women who get their ankles wet and lie awake all night with rheumatism.

RAHAB. I thought it was the Israelites that kept you awake.

SHUAH. Them and the rheumatism between them. Though I *will* say that the rheumatism lets up in the day time, but the very sight of those little black tents on the hills [*she pauses in the*

25

process of stamping herself into her shoes to peer through the little window at the country-side] makes my heart run up into my throat. [*She stands a moment, silent and intent, fascinated by the sight of the enemy*] Do you see that little white thing in the middle. Jabin the wine-seller told me that that is their holy place. They carry it about with them, he says, and as long as they have it with them they can do anything. Anything!

RAHAB. Except cross a flooded river and take a walled town.

SHUAH. They have magic that will part the river in two, Jabin says. The water goes solid like glass and breaks in two, and they just walk across.

RAHAB. Perhaps they can fly, too. [*She has not moved from her reclining position on the bed.*]

SHUAH. You may laugh, but everyone knows that they are sitting up there in the hills preparing magic to overwhelm us.

RAHAB. I hope they like the view of our palm-trees. It must be very dreary up there in the rain. [*In good-natured impatience*] How you love making a sensation, Shuah! What can a pack of sheep-grazers and cow-herds do against Jericho?

RAHAB. I don't know. There are so many of them. The hills are covered with them.

RAHAB. They are covered with gnats too. Stop peering at the country-side, and get us some food.

SHUAH. [*Coming away from the window and picking up a basket*] Food, indeed. My appetite runs away back into my teeth every time I remember them. I think: before another meal-time comes perhaps Jericho will be ashes and I shall be a cinder, a little, little cinder, among——

RAHAB. [*Not listening*] Get a pair of ducklings for supper.

SHUAH. [*Coming to earth at once*] We can't afford duckling.

RAHAB. Two plump, tender, juicy ones. [*Waving SHUAH away*] They will take the taste of those thousand years out of my mouth. If one isn't able to comfort the spirit one can pamper the flesh. [*As SHUAH is going out ; in business-like tones*] And don't pay Hoham for those olives. They were bad.

> SHUAH *goes out, turns to her left, and disappears down the rough terrace which makes a sloping path to the street below.*

RAHAB, *after a pause, rises in leisurely fashion, and moves
over to the mirror, adjusting her clothes and her hair.
At the mirror her absent-mindedness changes suddenly
into attention as she becomes aware of her identity.
She pauses.*

RAHAB. Ducks! [*Her chin tilts back in silent mockery*] You
poor fool. [*Considering it*] Kings have conquered and died and
been forgotten : why should you cry out against oblivion ? A
million million have lived happily and gone down into the dust
uncaring. And you make your short time bitter with rebellion.
[*She begins to make up her face with an absent-minded expertness.
Desisting suddenly*] It may be something I eat. I must watch.
Melon, perhaps. [*She picks up a pencil and begins to touch up her
eyebrows*] No. [*She pauses again*] It is a kind of sight. One sees
it like that, clear and plain. " Look, Shuah, look ! " But Shuah
sees nothing. She has a different kind of sight. Shuah doesn't
mind that she is no more important than that pencil. [*She
considers it*] Every day a little less and then—nothing. Nothing
any more. [*She drops the pencil on to the table as if it burns her.*]

*As she turns back to the room, there is the sound of a far-
away commotion in the town. It grows nearer, and
while it is still distant there is the sound of running feet
in the silence outside. The footsteps come rapidly
nearer, and two men run past the doorway from right to
left. The second man has hardly passed when the first
pauses, arrests the flight of the second, and drags him
into the room. Both flatten themselves against the back
wall, right, and await the coming of the pursuit. The
elder, MAHLON, is a man of twenty-five to thirty ; the
younger, CARMI, a youth of nineteen. RAHAB is standing against the wall between the mirror and the inner
door, and they are unaware of her presence.*

*Several soldiers run past, followed by a CAPTAIN. One
can hear the voices of the people as they come to roof-tops
and doors to call inquiries as to the trouble. The eddy
of excitement moves on for the moment, leaving the room
in comparative silence.*

MAHLON. It's a blind ending up there.

CARMI. Yes, they'll come back searching the houses.

RAHAB. [*In her rich, lazy voice*] That will be awkward for you.

> *Both men swing round.* CARMI'S *hand flies to the dagger at his waist, but* MAHLON'S *hand restrains him.*

MAHLON. Your pardon, lady. We thought the room was empty.

RAHAB. I am honoured. Your company is much sought after, it seems.

MAHLON. Lady, we are strangers here, and——

RAHAB. When your friends come back they can present you.

MAHLON. Two gold pieces if you hide us till they are gone.

RAHAB. Two ? Is my life priced at so little more than my favour ?

MAHLON. Three, then.

CARMI. Five ! All we have for ten minutes' shelter !

RAHAB. [*Dropping her mockery*] Why do they want you ?

CARMI. [*Into the moment's pause*] We—we stole some money from the inn-keeper.

RAHAB. [*Slowly*] Stole ? Since when have thieves held themselves like soldiers ?

CARMI. [*Alarmed by her perspicacity ; rushing on*] It was not very much that we took. A small purse. And—and a bracelet.

RAHAB. [*After a pause*] Very well. For a price I will hide you.

MAHLON. You shall have every coin we have.

RAHAB. Keep the coin. [*Holding out her hand to* CARMI] I will take the bracelet.

> CARMI, *overcome by confusion, stands helpless, his glance going to the disapproving* MAHLON *and coming away again.*

RAHAB. [*Withdrawing her hand with a contemptuous flick*] Never embroider a lie, my friend. It calls attention to it. Then if you are not thieves, what . . .

> *There is the sound of the search coming back. The* CAPTAIN *can actually be heard saying :* You take that one. I shall speak to Rahab.

RAHAB. [*Picking up the top rugs on the bed ; to* CARMI] Lie flat. Quick !

> CARMI *flings himself to the ground on the far side of the bed, and* RAHAB *throws the rug across him.*

RAHAB. [*While she is busy with* CARMI; *to* MAHLON, *pointing to the inner room*] In there !

MAHLON *disappears into the further room.*

RAHAB *picks up some sewing from the table, and sits down on the bed with it.*

Enter the CAPTAIN. *He stands in the doorway, a hand on the doorpost, in familiar fashion.*

CAPTAIN. Good evening, Rahab.

RAHAB. [*Looking up and acknowledging his presence*] Captain. On the wall in daylight ? What will your wife say ?

CAPTAIN. I am looking for two Israelite spies. My men say they came this way.

RAHAB. Spies !

CAPTAIN. Have you seen anything of them ?

RAHAB. No.

There is a pause.

CAPTAIN. [*Thoughtfully*] It strikes me as odd that when every door and roof-top is filled with people watching the hunt, you sit inside and embroider.

RAHAB. Not embroidery, Captain ; mending. Since when have bazaar rumours and street fights interested Rahab ?

CAPTAIN. [*With a short laugh*] That's true. You always gave yourself the airs of a princess. [*Doubt invading him ; coming a step into the room*] All the same——

RAHAB. [*Instantly*] Stay and drink some wine. You must be thirsty after the chase.

CAPTAIN. [*Half reassured*] No. I must go back to my men. You are sure that you . . . [*His eyes roam doubtfully.*]

RAHAB. Then wait just a moment. I have something to show you. [*She beckons him in, and goes to the table between the mirror and the inner door*] The ear-rings you bade me buy. [*She takes them from a box*] Aren't they lovely ?

CAPTAIN. [*Not greatly interested*] Very charming.

RAHAB. I beat the price down until Sihon cried real tears. A whole afternoon we spent bargaining. Wait till you see how well they look on. [*At the mirror, putting the ear-rings on.*]

CAPTAIN. I can't wait, Rahab. I must go.

RAHAB. Oh, just a moment. They set off my eyes beautifully.

There isn't another pair like them in all Canaan. No, nor in Egypt either.

CAPTAIN. I'm glad you like them, but I must go. I'm afraid my men will let those fellows slip through their fingers.

RAHAB. [*Busy with the ear-rings*] Where could they slip to, even if they did ? The gates are closed, aren't they ?

CAPTAIN. Oh, yes, they won't escape from the city. But it would be galling to let one of the other officers have the glory of their capture. To-morrow night, perhaps ?

RAHAB. [*Still apparently engrossed in the jewels*] Look at the lights in them ! Very well, to-morrow night. Send some wine if you are coming. What I have will be finished by then. [*She follows him to the door, and stands there watching him go. After a pause ; drawing the curtain across the door*] They have gone. [*She whips the rug from the recumbent CARMI, who flings himself on his knees at her feet.*]

CARMI. How can I thank you ? What can I do to show my gratitude ? My life is yours.

> But RAHAB'S *eyes are on the inner door, where* MAHLON *is standing.*

MAHLON. [*Quietly*] Why did you do it ? You must know now that we have little money.

RAHAB. Perhaps. But I have a large curiosity. [*She is as quiet as he. Between these two there is an interest, almost an understanding, that is lacking between* RAHAB *and the more obvious* CARMI, *in spite of his youthful good looks*] The cow-herds breed men after all, it seems.

MAHLON. [*At a loss*] Cow-herds ?

RAHAB. So you plan to take Jericho.

MAHLON. We shall take it. God has promised that.

RAHAB. Which god ?

MAHLON. God. There is only one.

RAHAB. Your one.

MAHLON. Yes.

RAHAB. [*Amused*] Well [*pouring wine into a cup*], if he is as sure of himself as you are, perhaps he is right. On the other hand, he may not have heard about our walls. [*She offers the cup to* CARMI, *who is nearest her.*]

MAHLON. [*As* CARMI *hesitates*] Not wine. Have you bread ?

RAHAB. There is what Shuah baked this morning. [*Indicating the inner room*] Under the linen cloth.

MAHLON. Shuah ?

RAHAB. My maid. She is at market.

MAHLON. [*Reassured*] Oh. [*He goes into the inner room for the bread.*]

RAHAB. [*Sipping the wine ; to* CARMI] And what bribe, or what threat, induced a Caananite boatman to risk crossing Jordan as it is now ?

CARMI. Oh, we didn't cross in a boat ! We daren't. [*As* RAHAB *looks inquiring*] The man might have talked, you see. We swam the river.

RAHAB. [*Incredulous*] You . . . !

CARMI. At least, Mahlon swam and I held on to his belt. [*As* MAHLON *comes back with a flat platter of rolls*] This is Mahlon. My name is Carmi.

RAHAB. My name is Rahab. [*She shakes her head as* MAHLON *offers her the bread, and her eyes follow him as he goes to* CARMI] Are there many like you among the Israelites ?

MAHLON. [*As he and* CARMI *take their rolls and begin to eat*] Thousands. We were chosen by lot.

RAHAB. [*Maliciously ; a little stung by his unconscious magnificence*] Ah, well, in that case they will not miss you when you don't come back.

> CARMI *pauses in munching his bread, but* MAHLON *chews with equanimity.*

MAHLON. [*Conversationally*] What excellent bread ! It is kind of you to share it with us.

RAHAB. [*Dryly*] Entertainment is my business.

CARMI. But we *must* get back ! If we don't, our people will not know about the . . . [*He catches* MAHLON'S *look, and pauses.*]

RAHAB. About what ?

MAHLON. About the woman called Rahab who makes bread so well, and who must certainly be saved when we sack Jericho.

RAHAB. The bribe is a little—insubstantial.

MAHLON. It was no bribe, but a promise.

RAHAB. It is neither, Israelite. Just an empty boast. Not

for five hundred years has anyone sacked Jericho. What engines have you that will breach these walls ?

CARMI. We shall not need engines. Mahlon says that if the ground is shaken enough the foundations will——

MAHLON. [*Interrupting*] My friend talks too much. I promise you that in two weeks' time we shall take Jericho. And that you and your house shall be saved.

RAHAB. And what if two spies are hanged over the walls to-night, and no report goes back to the hills ?

MAHLON. [*With a slow shrug*] Our women will mourn a while ; our names will live for ever on the lips of our people ; and two more men will come. But Rahab will perish in the ruins of Jericho.

RAHAB. [*To herself more than to them*] " On the lips of your people."

MAHLON. You won't save your city by destroying us.

RAHAB. [*Almost testily ; as one occupied with other thoughts and impatient of interruption*] It is not my city. I was born in a hill village. [*Indicating the bandage of torn cloth on* MAHLON'S *forearm*] Is this an Israelite custom ?

CARMI. No, that is where the lion caught him.

RAHAB. Lion ?

CARMI. In the reeds by the river. We spent two days there ; waiting for a chance to cross. Full of snakes the place is, too. You step on a piece of wood ; it is a snake sleeping. You hear a wind in the reeds ; it is a snake moving. You think : At last my feet are warm ; and you find that a snake has coiled itself round them and that——

RAHAB. But—the lion ?

CARMI. Oh, yes.

MAHLON. [*Ironical ; half-amused, half-angry ; drawling*] Must you tell about the lion ?

CARMI. [*Abashed*] She asked me.

MAHLON. Oh, by all means let us not be tongue-tied guests.

> CARMI *is not encouraged by the tone, but* RAHAB, *who has moved to her mending materials on the table, looks encouragingly at him.*

RAHAB. Tell me.

CARMI. [*Beginning tentatively, but improving in enthusiasm as he goes on*] You see, Mahlon was watching while I slept——

MAHLON. [*Quickly*] It was Carmi's turn for sleep.

> RAHAB *looks half affectionately at him, and goes on rummaging in her basket for a piece of linen. When she finds a piece she tears it in strips.*

CARMI. And in the early morning he heard something moving in the undergrowth, and turned to watch. It might be someone tracking us. And there, all of a sudden, was a lion, in the act of springing on me where I was lying. And instead of shouting out, Mahlon, all in the instant, pushed me *to* the brute, and fell over me, so that the lion went right over us both in his leap. And before I was awake he had wrapped his leather cloak round his arm for a shield, and with that arm in the lion's mouth was stabbing the beast in the neck with his dagger. A dagger is all we have for weapon, you see, because we must look like ordinary travellers. I added my dagger to his, but by that time it was child's play. There wasn't a scratch on me, but Mahlon had that [*indicating the bandage*].

RAHAB. [*Taking a small jar from the chest between the bed and the window*] So you saved your friend's life? [*She comes to him with the strips of linen and the jar of ointment.*]

MAHLON. To very little purpose. [*In answer to* RAHAB'S *eyebrows*] His tongue will kill him. [*As* RAHAB *reaches for the wounded arm*] It is very well as it is, thank you. [*He moves the arm behind him.*]

RAHAB. [*Hanging her strips of linen over the other forearm, which he is still using to eat his bread*] Hold these. [*She reaches for the withdrawn arm.*]

MAHLON. I assure you it is a very slight affair, not worth so much——

RAHAB. [*Unbandaging the arm*] No one makes poems about a man who dies of blood-poisoning. [*As* MAHLON *submits*] And having avoided the snakes, and slain the lion, and swum the river, a walled town looked just like a sweetmeat booth, I suppose. How did you get in, by the way?

CARMI. We came in with the vegetable carts yesterday morning.

RAHAB. [*Pausing in rubbing a strip of linen in the ointment*] Yesterday ! You have been two days in town ? Where did you sleep last night ?

CARMI. We didn't sleep. We were examining the wa——
[*He stops abruptly, but too late.*]

> *There is a moment's silence, while she stands motionless and the men apprehensive. It is as if she had repeated audibly : The walls !*

MAHLON. [*As she resumes bandaging ; quickly, as if to oppose her suspicion and antagonism*] Why should a hill-woman care what happens to Jericho ?

RAHAB. [*Conversationally*] That ointment is good, but you are the first man who didn't wince at the bite of it.

MAHLON. You will be safe, and all your family.

RAHAB. [*Still bright and chatty*] And after a sleepless night, too.

MAHLON. There will be riches for you, riches you never dreamed of.

RAHAB. [*Pausing ; furious*] Are you inviting me to help sack my own town ?

MAHLON. It isn't yours. You said so.

RAHAB. It has been my home for sixteen years.

MAHLON. [*Incredulously*] Do you love the place ?

RAHAB. [*Dryly*] I can restrain my ardour. The taxes are iniquitous, and the Government as corrupt as any in Canaan . . .

MAHLON. Well, then !

RAHAB. [*Taking fire from his complacence*] But it is strong. And magnificent. And beautiful. Who are you to pull down beauty ? You, whose knowledge of building ends with a tent-pole ! Who are you to destroy palaces ? What do you, cow-herds, know of civilisation ? A locust swarm knows as much ! Have you ever planted a tree ? Or carved a doorway ? Or shaped a plough ? No ! You are like hail, stripping the blossom and caring nothing for the harvest. You are sand, blown in from the desert, that makes a new desert of all it meets. Because you have courage and a sword in your hand, do you think——

> *She breaks off abruptly. Steps can be heard coming up the terrace outside. As they come nearer CARMI backs to the window, right ; not because it is a means of escape,*

34

but to have a wall at his back; and takes the dagger from his belt, holding it, point backwards, in his clenched fist. MAHLON stays where he is, warily, his hand lying lightly on the hilt of his weapon. The steps go past and die away.

RAHAB. [*Who has been watching them; quietly*] No one will come in while the curtain is over the doorway.

MAHLON. We are from the desert, yes. But *this* is our country. We are no blind destroyers. We are sons come to claim our inheritance. Let the King of Jericho submit, and there will be no——

RAHAB. Submit! Your impudence rivals your courage! Why should the King turn craven the moment you shake your fist at him?

MAHLON. Because we are stronger than he is. And God has promised us the land.

RAHAB. God again. Well, they say that faith is worth two swords to a man without a shield. But faith will do little for a rabble without the means of——

CARMI. [*Roused from his bread-munching*] We are not a rabble! For forty years we have obeyed the law. A strict and jealous law, let me tell you. Our fathers lived straitly in a hard country, learning to forget the soft life in Egypt, so that they . . . No, not they, but we. So that we should one day come into the country that is ours.

MAHLON. Carmi is right. We were born in the desert, both he and I. We have never known any other life. But the land we lived for was Canaan. Our mothers sang to us about it before we could walk. Our fathers told the wonder of it about the camp-fires at night.

CARMI. They have long memories, our people. Even in Egypt, my uncle says, the songs they sang were their own songs. Tales of the old life in the green plain between the hills and the sea. Canaan is ours. We have come back to it, that is all.

RAHAB. [*Taking her thoughts from their busyness with a people's traditions*] You must forgive Canaan if the welcome is a little cool. Her memory is not so good as yours.

MAHLON. She will remember us henceforth.

RAHAB. I have no doubt. And when our palaces, and our palm-trees, and our temples are in ashes, how much richer will you be ?

MAHLON. The corruption of the cities will be gone with the smoke of them. We will build anew, build clean . . . [*Seeing* RAHAB'S *interruption coming*] Yes, even if we live in tents while we do it. It is not brick and mortar that will make us great, but the Law. One law for priest and potter ; one justice.

RAHAB. Some of us would prefer mercy to justice. It's a cold world you picture, Israelite. I shall keep my bright, corrupt, beautiful Jericho.

CARMI. [*Cheerful barbarian*] Make the most of it, Rahab. There is only a little time left. [*He takes another huge bite.*]

MAHLON. It *is* beautiful. [RAHAB *flings him a glance of appreciation*] But when you are old you will look at the new Canaan and remember only the cruelty, the greed, the——

RAHAB. [*Harshly ; arguing, it would seem, more with some part of herself than with* MAHLON] I should remember only that I had betrayed a city !

MAHLON. There is no betrayal in helping us to escape.

RAHAB. Do you think I am a fool ! Do you think I don't know that if you die to-night the secret of the walls dies with you, and Jericho is safe ? What you have found out I don't know, but I know that it is vital. [*Going close to* MAHLON ; *all her interest is in* MAHLON] I can read its importance in your eyes. Your tongue is aching now to tell the news to your leader in the hills. And you ask me to help you escape !

> *As she pauses,* SHUAH'S *voice can be heard at some little distance outside. She is exchanging the time of day with a neighbour.* "Looks like rain again," *she is saying, although one cannot hear her distinctly.* "You been to market to-day ? What was the price of ducks ?" "Far too much," *says the neighbour.* "Eh ? What did you say ?" "Far too much !" "Yes, everything is six times the price it ought to be ! I thought it was because I was marketing late, but if it was the same with you in the morning . . ." *And so forth. The conversation goes on, far away, while the others talk.*

RAHAB. [*At the first sound of the voice*] Shuah !

MAHLON. Tell her that we are friends.

RAHAB. The whole of Jericho knows your description. And Shuah hates the invader. [*Referring to the distant cackle*] She has a silly voice, but she is no fool.

CARMI. You saved us once when you had nothing to gain. Now it is your life as well as ours that you save.

RAHAB. I won't do it. Am I to live the rest of my life with all Canaan—["*pointing fingers at me*" *she is going to say, but her passionate sweep of the arm at "all Canaan" has upset the things on the table. Her eyebrow pencil rolls to the floor. She stoops to pick it up, and straightens slowly, staring at the pencil.*]

CARMI. [*In an agony of impatience*] What does a broken pencil matter ! Don't you understand, you will live when Jericho is ashes.

> *She stares at him for a moment, as if his words meant more to her than he knows.*

RAHAB. [*Slowly*] Yes. I *would* live when . . . [*Collecting herself*] In there, a ladder goes to the roof. [*She indicates the inner room*] On the roof there is flax laid out in bundles. Enough to cover you. In half an hour it will be dark. There is a rope there that will reach the ground——

MAHLON. [*With quick suspicion*] A rope ?

RAHAB. My—clients sometimes go that way. Go quickly. She talks, but not for ever.

CARMI. [*Taking both her hands and raising them to his forehead*] Till we come again, Rahab. My life is twice yours. I shall not forget. [*He goes.*]

MAHLON. Nor shall I forget. You called it a boast that I made to you, but before God it is a promise and I shall redeem it.

RAHAB. [*Detaining him*] One thing before you go. It may be that when you come I shall not be here——

MAHLON. [*Puzzled*] Not——?

RAHAB. [*Lightly*] The God who promised you Jericho made no promises to me. Let the Captain but dream that I had tricked him, and . . . [*She lifts a shoulder, expressively*] Swear to me, then, that even if I am no longer here you will remember my name. That Rahab, who lived on the wall, saved you alive and gave Jericho into your hands.

MAHLON. I shall remember.

RAHAB. [*Quietly ; considering him*] I think you will.

MAHLON. And now, tell *me* something. [*As* RAHAB *urges him to go*] No, I must know.

RAHAB. Well ?

MAHLON. Why do you let us go ? Not out of fear ; you are a brave woman. Nor for revenge ; you don't hate Jericho. Then, why ?

RAHAB. For your bright eyes, my dear.

MAHLON. [*Refusing the explanation, almost angrily*] No, not for love. You have known too many men.

RAHAB. You are clever, Israelite ; most men would have been vain enough . . . Listen, then. If I gave you up, to-night, my reward would be a few gold pieces, spent to-morrow. If I let you go, your children's children will make songs about me.

MAHLON. I don't understand.

RAHAB. [*Briskly*] No. How should you ? [*As the conversation in the distance ceases*] Go. She is coming. [*As he disappears ; going after him to the inner door*] What is my name ?

MAHLON. [*Off*] Rahab.

      RAHAB *nods, satisfied. She comes slowly down to the little window giving on the country-side to look at the distant enemies who will make her immortal. She is standing there when* SHUAH *comes in.*

SHUAH. Robbers ! That's what they are ! Robbers !

RAHAB. [*Startled*] Who are ?

SHUAH. Everything double the price because of the war ! As if ducks stopped breeding because the Israelites are in the hills ! And leeks too. I suppose the leeks just give up growing through shock. A pack of thieves every one of them. There is the change. It is going to rain again, and the damp is in all my bones. [*Pausing to look at* RAHAB] Are you ill ?

RAHAB. No, of course not. [*The tone says : Why ?*]

SHUAH. You haven't counted your change. This day-dreaming of yours is growing into a disease. What have you done all the time I've been gone? Nothing, I'll be bound.

RAHAB. [*Slowly, almost incredulous*] I have overcome those thousand years.

SHUAH. [*With a glance at her; shrugging*] I don't know what you're talking about. [*Making for the inner room*] Shall I cook the ducks in a pot, or over the fire?

CURTAIN

THE MOTHER OF MASÉ

CHARACTERS

In order of appearance

YOHEB.	MASÉ.
HETSHEPSUT.	ARON.
LADY-IN-WAITING.	

A first-floor terrace in Thebes, about the year 1500 B.C. Although it is part of one of the palaces of the Eighteenth Dynasty it might, to look at, be the terrace of any modern block of luxury flats. The parapet, running along the back and overlooking an unseen courtyard below, is punctuated with small green trees in tubs. Right, the jutting wall of the house, with a door giving on to the terrace. Left, two pillars supporting the second storey, but giving free access to the rest of the terrace, which continues away to the left out of sight.

By the parapet are bench-like seats; and immediately down from it a table, with, right of it, a chair. Working at the table is YOHEB, a still, dark woman of middle age. She is goffering a pile of transparently fine linen garments. The linen is heaped in a basket, and her goffering irons are heated in a small brazier by her side.

Over everything is the clear Egyptian light.

Enter from the doorway HETSHEPSUT, ruling princess of Egypt, followed by a very young LADY-IN-WAITING. HETSHEPSUT is one of those good-natured, handsome, managing women who are dressed by the best houses and continue to ruin their couturier's work by hanging and pinning on themselves irrelevant but favoured possessions. The kind of woman whose handbag is invariably a shapeless reticule containing everything but a Bradshaw. Her wig is brilliant, beautifully curled, but very faintly out of the plumb; and the general effect of her very lovely clothes is one of vague untidiness. A woman, in fact, too full of other interests, and too sure in any case of her abundant charm, to care what she looks like.

At the moment she is carrying an armful of freshly cut flowers. She is talking as she comes, so that one hears her approach some distance away. As she comes in, YOHEB pauses in her work to give an automatic obeisance.

HET. [*Hailing* YOHEB] Ah, good morning, Yoheb ! [*To the* LADY-IN-WAITING] Take the flowers, child, and begin the garland. I shall come presently. [*Indicating the farther terrace*] There is a table over there. [*As the girl goes*] And use a little taste as well as industry ! [*To the world at large*] A good child, but without the light of the spirit. [*Moving over to* YOHEB] How are you this morning, Yoheb ?

YOHEB. [*With the impersonal glance of long intimacy*] It is a strange thing how your highness makes a good piece of goffering look like a rag in fifteen minutes.

HET. It is hot in the garden, even so early. And anyhow, what do clothes matter ? [*Subsiding thankfully on to the chair*] It is good to be in the garden again, after a week of the Council Chamber. What fools men are when they get together ! They would sacrifice a province for the sake of scoring off a rival in debate.

YOHEB. [*Goffering with detachment*] They are all as some woman made them.

HET. I refuse to believe that any woman made the Chief Secretary. He is merely Stupidity become visible. As for the High Priest . . .! Oh, well ! [*Dismissing them*] They can annoy their wives for the rest of the month. [*As the comfortable silence settles about them ; calmly*] Where is he this morning, Yoheb ? [*She has not accented the pronoun. " He " is obviously their chief interest and normal subject of conversation.*]

YOHEB. [*With a slight backward movement of her head, which indicates that the affair is taking place somewhere below*] He is playing hand-ball with the Chamberlain's sons. [*After a short pause*] He will come in presently to say that he has won.

HET. [*Answering some unspoken criticism*] It is good to win !

YOHEB. But not to boast about it.

HET. What is troubling *you* this morning, Yoheb ?

YOHEB. He is.

41

HET. [*Unbelieving*] Masé! [*Quickly*] He's not ill, is he?

YOHEB. [*Reassuring*] No, highness, no.

HET. Well, then! You know very well that Masé has never given us a moment's care since that day I found him among the reeds. [*Reminiscent, amused*] Red with crying and very angry. It was hot in that little box. Fifteen years, Yoheb; and never a bad moment. Would that all adoptions turned out so well! And now you fret yourself into a sweat on a hot morning because he likes to win games.

YOHEB. No one boasts who is master of himself. He is not a child any longer, to need praise from others.

HET. [*Conceding*] Perhaps his stammer keeps him backward a little. We might consult the doctors about him, if they were not a pack of fools.

YOHEB. It is not magic he needs, but a new life.

HET. Oh, well; next year he will be sixteen and of age, and we can marry him to some nice girl. That will be interesting for him.

YOHEB. It might be wiser to wait.

HET. [*In a new voice; simply*] Are you disappointed in your son, Yoheb? [*She means: In what I have made of your son.*]

YOHEB. No, highness, no. But I am—anxious. [*With a simplicity to match her mistress's; as one woman to another*] I think we have spoiled him, between us.

HET. [*Recovering her poise*] You think *I* have spoiled him, 'm? Well, perhaps I have. Does it matter so much? He is happy; he is charming; he has a head full of learning, a good ear for music, and a good eye for the bow; he is mightily handsome and sufficiently popular. What more do you want him to be?

YOHEB. I should like him to be a man. [*Tentatively*] It would be a good thing, perhaps, if he were to be sent away.

HET. [*Amazed and a little indignant*] Sent away from Thebes? From me! [*More kindly*] Away from you, Yoheb?

YOHEB. But for the grace of Yahveh and your highness's charity I would not have had him these fifteen years. When I put him out on the river-bank I had not hoped for happiness like that. Who am I that I should keep him now from a wider life beyond the Court?

HET. So you want to put him out on the river-bank again—all for his own good ? Well, perhaps he *has* been too long at Court. A little travel would do him no harm. There is an embassy going to Kadesh next month ; he might go with that. Embassies are very broadening for the mind—if a little hard on the stomach. And he would have a pleasant time.

YOHEB. [*A little more dryly than she had intended*] Yes, he would have a pleasant time.

HET. [*Annoyed*] You, then, *you* suggest something, since you are so anxious to see him go.

YOHEB. [*Calmly, but not finding it easy now that it has come to the point*] The King is sending an expedition to Nubia. It might be a good thing if he were to see some service.

HET. Go to the war !

YOHEB. Go with the army.

HET. I won't hear of it ! [*As* YOHEB *says nothing*] Have you spoken of this to him ?

YOHEB. No, highness.

HET. I forbid you to mention it.

YOHEB. Yes, highness.

HET. I forbid you even to hint at it. An outrageous suggestion ! Have I trained the boy in every princely talent to have a Nubian arrow bring it all to nothing ! And *you* ; how can you stand there calmly and propose to send him into danger ?

YOHEB. I sent him away once before, when he was less able to take care of himself.

HET. But that was to save him from greater danger ; from massacre. This is wanton !

YOHEB. He will not be killed. I know that in my heart. He will be a great prince, my son. But not until he can stand up in the light and look men and gods in the face. In Nubia he will not be any longer Masé, prince of Egypt. He will be no better than his own right arm, and his own will. And when he finds that these don't fail him, he will find himself. That is worth some danger—and some lying awake of nights.

HET. [*Considering her*] And I thought that *I* loved him ! *Her mind going from* YOHEB'S *spiritual characteristics to her*

43

physical ones] I think sometimes that he grows very like you, Yoheb. It is a wonder that he doesn't notice.

YOHEB. One doesn't see the people one lives with.

HET. And he still has never asked about his parentage ?

YOHEB. Never, highness.

HET. That is strange, isn't it ? He must be curious.

YOHEB. I think he takes it for granted that if you knew, highness, you would have told him.

HET. You have been a faithful servant to me, Yoheb. And I should like to do something for you. If the boy ever asks, shall we tell him the truth ?

YOHEB. [*Instantly ; shocked*] No ! No, highness.

HET. But you would be quite safe now. My father is dead, and no one in these days would prosecute you for having kept your child alive. Even if they did, you have my protection. I am Egypt now—whatever my husband may say.

YOHEB. I wasn't thinking of myself. Not that way, at least.

HET. As for Masé, we have never made any secret of his Hebrew blood. It would be no shock to him.

YOHEB. Who knows ? We are a very poor family ; very undistinguished, as your highness is aware. He may have pictured finer things for himself. There are prosperous people even among the Hebrews.

HET. Hezron the banker, for instance ? Dripping with money and bloated with good living ? Don't you think that any boy would be proud of a mother who risked her life to keep him alive ? Who left her home and her family so that after all he might not be brought up by strangers ? [*As* YOHEB *does not speak*] Is it possible that you don't *want* the boy to know ?

YOHEB. There is nothing I want less, highness.

HET. But it is I who would be the loser, once he knew. If I don't mind, why should you ?

YOHEB. He loves me now. But he loves me for what I am : the woman who taught him how to lace his first outdoor shoes, the woman who binds his cut finger and holds his head when he is sick. I could not bear to see him look at me differently ; as if I were a stranger, perhaps. It would——

HET. But—but have you thought of him ? You say he lacks

44

confidence, that he doesn't know how to deal with the world. It might be a happier thing to know one's parents than to think of oneself as a waif.

YOHEB. [*Unhappily; considering it*] Yes, there is that. But I couldn't. I couldn't face losing the love I have from him now ; and having nothing to put in its place, perhaps. I would do much for him, but not that. Let us not even think of it, highness. Please, highness, if I have served you in anything, let me have your word that you will never——

HET. [*Soothing*] Very well, Yoheb, very well. He shall not know ; if that is how you would have it. [*Briskly resuming the former subject*] But I forbid you to mention going to the war to him.

YOHEB. [*In a toneless submission that does not hide her opinion*] Yes, highness.

HET. [*Unable to bear the unspoken criticism ; airily*] If the subject is to be brought up at all, it is for me to speak of it.

YOHEB. [*Carefully ignoring any capitulation*] Yes, highness.

HET. If he wanted very much to go, that might be different. Something might be arranged. But only to the base, of course.

YOHEB. Yes, highness.

HETSHEPSUT, *becoming aware of the two of them and their solemn farce, utters a short bark of a laugh.*

HET. [*In grim amusement*] Women ! I thought that men were fools, but they are not fools enough to hurt themselves. [*In business-like tones, as the memory comes back to her ; and glad enough to carry the war into* YOHEB's *country*] Talking of women, I hear that daughter of yours has been making a fool of herself again.

YOHEB. Miriam was always headstrong.

HET. [*Feeling that " headstrong " does not meet the case at all*] But, preaching sedition in the market-place ! Can't Aron do something to stop her ? A nice sensible creature ! He will lose his very good post in the Office of Works if she goes on like this. What ails her ?

YOHEB. Well, you see, highness, there is a prophecy among my people.

HET. Prophecies are two for a groat.

YOHEB. It is foretold that after four hundred years we should leave Egypt and go back to Syria.

HET. What, all of you !

YOHEB. Yes, highness, every one. And the four hundred years are nearly up.

HET. And what power is going to make Hezron the banker join with Shimi the bricklayer in a jaunt to Syria ?

YOHEB. The prophecy says that when the time comes a leader will come too ; to unite the people. That is what moves Miriam. She says that the Hebrews must be prepared, for at any moment now the man whose destiny it is to lead them will appear.

HET. Don't tell me *you* believe such nonsense !

But the end of the sentence is lost in the arrival of MASÉ, *who comes in, breathless and radiant, from the terrace, left ; the stitched leather ball he has been playing with still in his hand.*

MASÉ. I've won !

MASÉ *is everything that* HETSHEPSUT *has claimed for him ; he is also everything that* YOHEB *said he was. His remark is addressed to* YOHEB, *but now he catches sight of the princess, sitting in the chair beyond.*

MASÉ. Mother ! [*He goes to her, pleased. Greeting her*] How good to find you here ! I haven't seen you for an age. Five days—six days ? How was the Council ?

HET. Much as usual. You must come to the next, I think. It is time you took an interest in affairs.

MASÉ. Oh, I am never going to be a man of affairs. I shall lead a nice quiet life writing your letters for you, and [*with a light caress to take any sting from the words*] being thankful that I am not your heir, princess. I should hate speechifying——

HET. There is no need to " speechify "——

MASÉ. And I lose my temper when I am contradicted, and that is fatal in a statesman.

YOHEB. [*Goffering*] One could, of course, learn to keep one's temper.

He makes a face at her.

HET. But since you obviously cannot make a career of writing my letters——

46

MASÉ. Why not ? I make up much better lies than you do.

HET. —we must find a medium for you.

MASÉ. [*Lightly ; anxious to shelve the subject*] If it is all the same to you, I should like to be a charioteer.

HET. The professionals might object.

MASÉ. Then, failing that, a flute-player.

HET. Have I raised you in all the wisdom of the ages to have you joining a concert party ? [*Seriously*] The Prime Minister was suggesting yesterday that you might make one of his staff for a little, and learn something about administration.

MASÉ. [*With seeming irrelevance*] I have just been playing with Senmut's nephew. [*It is obvious that Senmut is the Prime Minister*] He is going with the first draft to Nubia to-morrow.

HET. Oh ? [*Avoiding* YOHEB'S *eye*] I—er—suppose you wouldn't like to go with him ?

MASÉ. Go with him ! To the war ? [*Ecstatic*] Oh, that would be glorious ! [*Surprised*] Would you let me go ? [*Punctured*] But I should be no g-good as a soldier. I d-don't know anything ab-bout it ; and I should stammer when it came to command.

HET. But you just tell the under-officers to do what they usually do. That is all being in the army is.

MASÉ. In peace, perhaps. But n-not in battle. One would have to be sure, then ; and quick. I should be no good. I should only disgrace myself ; and you. You had better allow me to write your letters, beloved.

YOHEB. The princess might let you go as an ordinary soldier ; without a command.

MASÉ. Don't be ridiculous, Yoheb. Of *course* I couldn't go as an ordinary soldier !

HET. [*With a glance at* YOHEB, *who refuses to meet her eye*] Well. That seems to be that. We must . . . [*Her eye going on from* YOHEB *to the distant* LADY-IN-WAITING, *and horror invading her countenance as she takes in the enormity of the* LADY-IN-WAITING'S *handiwork*] No, no, *no*, child ! [*Rising as her voice rises ; in anyone but the majesty of Egypt it would be a yell*] *Not* the marigolds ! [*To the others*] A sweet child, but gods and gods ! what a fool ! [*She rushes out to the rescue.*]

47

YOHEB. [*After a pause, to* MASÉ *lounging beside her*] You had better change that tunic, hadn't you ? It must be damp after your game.

MASÉ. [*Not moving; in a new voice, unconsciously more intimate than the tone he has used to the princess*] Yoheb, do you think perhaps they *let* me win ?

YOHEB. [*Matter-of-factly*] Why should they ?

MASÉ. Because I am the prince.

YOHEB. Don't you play well ?

MASÉ. Yes, I suppose so.

YOHEB. Well, then.

HET. [*Off*] Use a little common sense, my dear sweet child ; and a modicum of taste.

MASÉ. [*Watching her; amused*] She is lovely, isn't she ?

YOHEB. Who ? Nini ?

MASÉ. No. My mother.

YOHEB. [*After a moment*] You love the princess very dearly, don't you ?

MASÉ. [*As who should say : What a silly question*] Of course.

YOHEB. [*Feeling like someone stepping into the sea for the first time, and not knowing how deep it was*] Have you ever wondered about your own mother ?

MASÉ. [*Airily*] Oh, I know all about that.

YOHEB. [*Astounded*] You know !

MASÉ. It was a clever idea, the box in the reeds, wasn't it !

YOHEB. [*At a loss for words*] Well, I . . . It seemed the obvious thing at the time, I suppose.

MASÉ. [*Rather pleased to have surprised her*] Did you really believe that I should not hear the Court gossip ? Or that I could look in a mirror and not see the foreigner in my face ? The very shape of my bones is Syrian. Did you know my father ?

YOHEB. Did I know whom ?

MASÉ. The Syrian prince my mother loved. She must have loved him greatly to risk a scandal for his sake. Did you know him, Yoheb ?

YOHEB. [*Slowly*] No. No.

MASÉ. But you were there when I was born, weren't you ?

YOHEB. Yes, I was there.

48

MASÉ. And he didn't come to see me ? Or to see my mother ?

YOHEB. No Syrian prince came to your cradle, my son.

MASÉ. Of course, being a hostage, he might not have been free. And there was the scandal to avoid. Very neatly it was avoided too, wasn't it ? Finding me on the river-bank ! Not that it fooled anyone, but it did make things easier, I suppose. And the trouble about the Hebrews' children gave someone the idea. Whose idea was it : the chest of papyrus and the finding in the reeds ?

YOHEB. It was mine.

MASÉ. What ! Well, who would have thought that my staid, upright, stolid Yoheb had such guile in her ! I shall remember that next time you preach behaviour to me.

YOHEB. [*Not knowing whether she is glad or sorry that the subject is settled for her*] You had better change that tunic.

MASÉ. [*Not listening*] And here, if I am not mistaken, comes your staid, upright, stolid son. [*They watch the arrival of someone on the farther terrace*] I like Aron. You have a nice family, Yoheb. How did anything so attractive come out of a worthless race like the Hebrews ?

> Before YOHEB *can answer,* HETSHEPSUT *comes back with* ARON *in tow.* ARON *is handsome, dignified, intelligent, and grown-up. Indeed, though still a young man he has been grown-up for a long time. He has neither the temperament nor the doubts that make* MASÉ *such a problem to himself and to his elders. If his normal self-confidence is a little impaired at the moment, the fact is hardly apparent.*

HET. Look ! I've brought you a visitor, Yoheb.

MASÉ. Good morning, Aron.

ARON. [*With an obeisance*] Good morning, highness.

YOHEB. How are you, my son ?

MASÉ. Aron, will you show me again how you get that back-hand stroke ?

ARON. Surely, highness. With pleasure.

HET. What is all this I hear about Miriam ? Have you no control over her ? She really must not be allowed to make a fool of herself in public, or she will get you all into trouble.

ARON. It was about Miriam that I came. [*He pauses, uncertain.*]

HET. Yes ?

ARON. [*Looking from one to the other and playing for time ; he has not expected to run into* HETSHEPSUT] It is all very difficult. She has visions, you see, highness . . .

HET. Well, there is nothing intrinsically wrong with visions. Very good and commendable things in their proper place. But this public agitating—it must stop, Aron.

ARON. I wish I knew what to do. Could I, with your gracious highness's permission, speak to my mother alone ?

HET. Nonsense ! Your mother's family has been mine for fifteen years. And if it is about Miriam it is practically public business. So let us hear what is worrying you.

ARON. [*Comforting himself*] Well, your highness would hear it sooner or later, I suppose. It is like this, highness. Miriam had one of her turns last night. A bad one. And the results are likely to be embarrassing.

HET. It is no doubt epilepsy or something of the sort. I shall send a doctor to see her to-day. They are all fools, so it is not likely that he will cure her, but he will take the responsibility from your shoulders. So don't worry about it, my good Aron. No one shall blame you or your family.

ARON. [*Beginning to get desperate*] Your highness doesn't understand. [*Beginning again*] Your highness knows, perhaps, that my sister preaches the coming of a deliverer for the Hebrews. [HET. *assents.*] Very well ; last night she had a vision, or says she had, and in the vision it was revealed to her who the leader of our people is to be.

HET. And who is it ? [*Hopefully*] Not Hezron the banker, I suppose ? I would almost pay her a pension to embarrass that man.

ARON. No, highness. Not Hezron.

HET. Who, then ?

> MASÉ *has half turned to throw the ball he is holding to someone in the courtyard below.* ARON *turns his head slowly to look at him, and makes a helpless gesture in his direction.*

YOHEB. [*Quicker to understand than* HETSHEPSUT; *instantly repudiating*] No! [HETSHEPSUT *stares.*

MASÉ. [*Turning back from the parapet*] Who is it to be, Aron?

ARON. [*After a moment's pause*] My youngest brother, highness.

MASÉ. [*Lightly*] That savours of nepotism, doesn't it? A truly Hebrew sin: keeping it in the family. [*Seeing* YOHEB'S *face, and putting an arm across her shoulders in careless affection*] Don't mind, Yoheb. Nothing will come of it. [*To* ARON] I didn't know you had a brother. [*He is not greatly interested.*]

ARON. He left home when he was very young, highness.

MASÉ. [*To* YOHEB, *giving her a friendly squeeze*] That was when you came to us, 'm? Well, I am glad that Miriam's choice fell on him and not on you, Aron. I should hate to see you made into a figurehead for a rabble.

ARON. [*Stung by " rabble "*] If the time were to come, I should make a better job of it than my brother.

HET. [*Her political sense alert even now*] If the time came! [*Coldly*] Do I understand that you consider it a possibility?

ARON. My sister's visions may be dreams, highness, but the whips on the backs of the Hebrew labourers are real enough.

HET. But it is Hebrews who do the whipping.

ARON. To please Egyptian masters.

MASÉ. Senmut says that a Hebrew would flog his grandmother for a groat.

ARON. [*Restraining himself; he has not meant to make that remark about being a better leader than* MASÉ] The Prime Minister has a weakness for a phrase.

HET. If you read a little history, my good Aron, you would know that there was no cruelty in Egypt until you Syrians brought it with you. It is a little late to be righteous about it. However, for Egypt's good I shall cause inquiry to be made. In the meantime, Miriam's tongue must be stopped. You understand? [*The last phrase is a warning rather than a question; authority might ignore the vague prophecies of a madwoman, but the adopted son of the Princess of Egypt must on no account be compromised.*]

ARON. Does your highness propose to cut it out ? [*As* HETSHEPSUT *pauses to examine his tone, not sure whether there is offence in it or not ; smoothly*] No one deplores the unsuitability of Miriam's visions more than your servant, gracious highness, but I have no power over her. She is possessed. Nothing but death would ever silence her.

YOHEB. [*In appeal to* HETSHEPSUT] Highness . . .

HET. Be assured, Yoheb. There is no question of that. Some other means must be found.

ARON. My brother might be sent away.

YOHEB. Yes.

ARON. There would be no following for an absent leader. Even Miriam might lose heart——

HET. Yes, that might be wise.

MASÉ. It is a little sad for your brother to be bundled out of Egypt just because Miriam wants to be sister to a hero ! I take it that *he* has no yearnings to unite Israel ?

ARON. [*Growing frayed*] There is no saying what folly he might commit.

YOHEB. [*Warning*] Aron !

ARON. It is a heady thing to speak for a people. Even your highness might one day show an interest in the Hebrews.

MASÉ. No. They don't wash enough.

ARON. They lack your highness's scented baths.

MASÉ. So do *my* people, most of them ; but they find water enough.

ARON. Your people—highness ?

MASÉ. The Egyptians. We wash, my dear Aron ; rich or poor. I could never be sorry for a dirty skin.

ARON. [*Who, what with Miriam and her misplaced revelations, is rapidly finding life not worth living ; furious*] And is your own skin become so thick, highness, that no Hebrew blood shows through ?

MASÉ. [*Taken aback*] I think you are being insolent. And if what you say has any meaning, I fail to understand it.

HET. [*Her mind divided between* ARON'S *unexpected bad manners and* MASÉ'S *Egyptian boastings*] What is all this about Egyptian——

YOHEB. [*Interposing hastily, in warning*] His highness has heard Court gossip that your highness is his mother.

HET. [*Not realising how much is involved*] They give me too much credit.

MASÉ. [*After a staggered pause*] You mean that you are *not* my mother ? [*As* HETSHEPSUT'S *face, losing its smile now that the seriousness of the situation is becoming apparent, makes it obvious that she is not*] You mean that I was truly a foundling ? [*As the thing begins to come home to him*] A *Hebrew* brat ? [HET. *begins to speak, but he turns to* YOHEB, *accusing*] But you said you were there ! You said it was you who thought of the box . . . [*Before he has finished the word " box " the implication is clear to him; in a dull voice*] Oh. [*Looking from one to another, and, because each of the three is momentarily at a loss, for once dominating them*] Did you have to lie to me ?

HET. No one lied to you, my dear.

MASÉ. [*Overriding her attempt to speak*] Why could I not have been told ! Did it please you to see me making a fool of myself ? Playing the prince——

HET. [*Determined that he shall listen*] Be reasonable, darling ! Yoheb could have been put to death for having kept you alive. That was ample——

MASÉ. Why did she ? Aren't there enough Hebrew brats in Egypt ? [*To* ARON] And you. I suppose you have been enjoying me for a long time. [*Mimicking* ARON'S *respectful voice*] " Your highness knows best " ; " As your highness wishes " ; " Delighted, your highness, any time ".

ARON. I have never mocked you, even in my mind. No, nor envied you. If I have spent emotion on you, it was to be sorry that so much glory was hung on so poor a frame. If the rest of Israel cannot wear prosperity any better than that, they had best remain in bondage. [*To* HETSHEPSUT, *hurriedly*] Forgive me, gracious highness, for anything I may have said, and permit me to leave your presence. [*Exit.*]

MASÉ. [*Viciously*] It is to be hoped that his brother has more charm, or he will do little with the sons of Israel. [*Struck by a new thought*] I suppose he *has* a brother ?

YOHEB. Only you, my son.

MASÉ *utters a short, unamused laugh.*

MASÉ. Does Miriam really believe that I would lead the Hebrews in a revolution ?

YOHEB. [*Quiet and dry*] If she does, she is going to be disappointed. So far, you are incapable of leading a half-company of mercenaries to Nubia.

HET. [*Kindly*] Let him be, Yoheb. He has had enough for the moment.

YOHEB. This *is* the moment, highness. [*To* MASÉ] Who are you to despise the Hebrews ? The very poorest of them is more to be reverenced than you. There is not one of them but takes his few pence with courage—and saves the odd coin for a feast day. What do you know of courage ? It may not be a lovely thing to cart mud for a living, but to sing at the carting is lovely. To look men and gods in the face and be glad.

MASÉ. Do you want me to carry a hod, perhaps ?

YOHEB. [*Not heeding*] I gave you life. Twice I gave you life. The princess gave you learning and a great place. By some mystery of God you are a prince of Egypt ; and what are you besides ? If you are crossed, you sulk ; if you lose a game, you are at the point of death ; if your nose bleeds it is the end of the world.

HET. You make too much of it, Yoheb.

YOHEB. Perhaps it is I who have bred a weakling. Or perhaps the air of Courts is thinning to Hebrew blood. If you had worked in the fields or the brickyards like your fellows, or herded sheep in the desert like your fathers, you might have grown up, who knows. Might have been master of yourself and master of men because of it. I only know that in a world full of danger and challenge and achievement the son I bore proposes to spend his manhood answering someone else's invitations to supper.

MASÉ. [*Furious*] You think I am a coward ?

YOHEB. What else ?

HET. You do the boy injustice, Yoheb.

> *But neither is listening to, nor aware of, her. The issue is between them, and they have forgotten outsiders.*

MASÉ. You think I am afraid to go to Nubia, afraid of being killed ?

YOHEB. Oh, no. Being killed is the last thing you think of. You are afraid of not being good enough ; afraid of new experience ; afraid of responsibility ; of being ridiculous ; of being hurt ; of being left out of things ; of being let in for things, of being——

MASÉ. Stop it !

YOHEB. —supplanted while you are gone. Is there anything in heaven or earth that you are not frightened of, my son ?

MASÉ. Don't call me that ! I hate you ! I wish you had killed me when you bore me, as you were ordered to. I shall go to the war, and go gladly ! I shall see Senmut now and he will let me go with the draft to-morrow. I will show them that the son of sheep-herds can fight as well as any rice-fed Nile brat. Yes, and die as well ! [*Spoiling the effect of this excellent sentiment by a characteristic return to childishness*] And when I am dead perhaps you will all be sorry ! [*He rushes out by the door, right.*]

HET. [*Moving as if to follow him, distressed*] What have you done !

YOHEB. [*Calmly*] You said that he might go.

HET. But not like that ! He will do some desperate thing. He will be killed in that barbarous country.

YOHEB. [*Restraining her, more by her voice than by her gesture*] No, highness. I have said he will live ; and he will come back a man. He will be a great prince, my son.

She reaches for the goffering, to pile it into the basket.

HETSHEPSUT, *about to hurry after* MASÉ, *changes her mind as her interest shifts to* YOHEB. *She stands arrested, looking back at her servant, as the curtain falls.*

CURTAIN

SARA

CHARACTERS

In order of appearance

HAGAR.	MILCAH.
SARA.	ABRAHAM.
LOT.	

A room in Ur, about 2000 B.C. Ur is civilised, elegant, and old. The room is civilised, elegant, and not too new. There is an air of coolness as contrasted with a great heat outside.

On a day bed SARA *lies resting, in undress. To her comes her maid,* HAGAR.

HAGAR. [*Softly*] Madam.

SARA. [*Rousing*] Hagar ? What is it ? It is not supper-time surely. The sun is quite high.

HAGAR. There is a visitor, madam. The master's nephew.

SARA. Lot ? What does he want ?

HAGAR. He wants to speak with you, madam.

SARA. With me ? Why not with Abraham ?

HAGAR. The master is not here.

SARA. [*Sharply*] Is Abraham not in the house ?

HAGAR. Instead of going to rest after lunch, he went out ; and he has not come back.

SARA. In this heat ? What can he be thinking of.

HAGAR. In any case it was for you that Lot asked.

SARA. [*Suddenly alarmed*] Has something happened—something that Lot has come to——

HAGAR. Oh, no, madam ; it is not bad news. Lot is quite undisturbed. He is eating sweets from your little silver dish.

SARA. Lot would eat sweets if his mother were dying. [*She is nevertheless reassured*] Oh, well. [*She begins to rise.*]

HAGAR. Shall I help you dress ?

SARA. No. Go and tell Lot that I shall see him. By the time

you have prised him away from the sweets I shall be ready. [*As* HAGAR *is going*] His wife is not with him, is she ?

HAGAR. No, madam.

SARA. Well, let us be thankful for small mercies. [HAGAR *goes.*] Lot, indeed. With the sun still above the horizon, and the town like a cauldron. It can't be to borrow money, or he would have asked for Abraham. And he can't have come to supper, or he would have brought that wife of his. And it can't be . . . [*she pauses for a moment as the fear clutches her*] can't be that anything has happened to Abraham. [*Refusing it*] No, it can't. If it were that he would have rushed in and roused the house and taken charge, as befits a distressed heir. Sara, my dear, you are becoming deplorably bitter. [*Glancing at her face in the mirror*] It is at least comforting that if you are well on the way to being a shrew, you still show no signs of becoming a hag. Being one of the best-looking women in Ur is no small compensation for the daily trials of life. Having Lot for a nephew, for instance. [*Enter* LOT, *shown in by* HAGAR, *who goes.*] Good-day to you, Lot. What has brought you so early of an evening ? There is nothing wrong, I hope ?

LOT. Aunt Sara, I do apologise for this intrusion. I know it is intolerable of me to curtail your rest on so hot a day. Indeed, nothing would have induced me to such a course if it had not been that I was so worried.

SARA. Worried ?

LOT. So worried that I could not sleep this afternoon. To be truthful I have not slept for nights, my mind was so troubled.

SARA. Is something wrong with your business again ?

LOT. *My* business ? Oh, no. Everything goes well there, thank the gods. What I am distressed about is my uncle.

SARA. Is it that bill he backed for you ?

LOT. Aunt Sara ! Can you never give me credit for a motive that is not personal !

SARA. My dear Lot, I do most humbly apologise. But you come to me with your worry, and so I take it to be a personal one.

LOT. It is a personal one. But not in that sense. It is about Abraham.

SARA. [*In natural tones, but somehow guarded*] And what worries you about Abraham?

LOT. He is behaving very strangely. So strangely that people are beginning to talk.

SARA. [*Ironic*] What a dreadful thing. And how is he strange?

LOT. He seems not to know what is said to him. He passes lifelong friends without a bow. If they call to him he stares through them. Only this morning the Surveyor met him, and stopped to tell him about that new drainage scheme they are planning. A big thing, it is; five hundred acres. And if it goes through there would be a lot in it for Abraham. And what do you think Abraham said?

SARA. What?

LOT. He just stared at the Surveyor and said: "Bricks. They are made from the mud and they go back to the mud. What are bricks to build with?" Aunt Sara, do you think he is losing his mind?

SARA. [*Guarded again; repressive*] I see no signs of it. He is a little absent-minded lately.

LOT. Absent-minded! There is a point where absent-minded-ness becomes criminal. Do you know that the King has suggested Abraham as being the ideal person to head the new Committee for the Improvement of Social Amenities. Do you know what that means? Do you know who will be on that Committee? Representatives of the Court, of the Temple, of the Army, of Big Business, and of the landowners. And who would be the man to keep the balance between them, to play one interest off against another, until the whole city revolved round him and every last bushel of wheat from the country and every last brick from the kiln was in his gift? Abraham! But if it is whispered that his mind is sick——

SARA. His mind is not sick.

LOT. [*Not heeding*] If they think his judgment no longer of account, there will be no place on that Committee for Abraham. It is the chance of a lifetime. Of a thousand lifetimes. And Abraham is liable to throw it away by his odd behaviour.

SARA. I don't see why it should be such a worry to *you*, Lot.

What Abraham may lose will be his own loss. His oddity harms no one but himself.

LOT. [*Pouncing*] Then you admit that he is behaving oddly ?

SARA. [*Smoothly*] Oh, yes. It does not need his *nephew* to tell me about my husband. And Abraham is more than my husband. He is my child too. He has not been well lately. He is absent-minded, and has bouts of rage and impatience. Not at all like himself. But I am hoping that when the cooler weather comes he may regain his old——

LOT. By the time the cooler weather comes that place on the Committee will be filled. And unless my uncle controls himself the place will not be filled by Abraham. That is why I came to see you ; when he was not here. I thought——

SARA. How did you know he was not at home ?

LOT. Because he is walking up and down under the trees on the north terrace.

SARA. [*Relieved*] Well, let us be thankful for the trees, at least.

LOT. He has been doing that all the afternoon, while even the hungry pariah dogs slept. So I took the chance of seeing you. I want you to use your influence with him. He is devoted to you ; and there is no one in the whole Euphrates valley who has one-half your charm and persuasive quality. He will listen to you.

SARA. Listen to what ?

LOT. Tell him that he owes it to his family to be more careful. That there are great successes ahead of him, and that it behoves him to show a little more interest, to make some effort——

SARA. For what ? [*As* LOT *pauses, at a loss for her meaning*] For what, I ask you ? To gain a little fresh honour ? He is already well thought of. To be the envy of the town ? He has never cared for such things. To buy me a new jewel ? I have already more than I can wear. Not a month goes by but he adds to the store. [*With a mixture of irony for the obtuseness of man and of tenderness for his childishness*] It is his way of comforting me for having no child. For what reason should I prod my weary husband into . . . [*She pauses. The voices of* HAGAR *and another woman are audible, off*] I think that is your wife's voice.

LOT. Yes, it does sound like Milcah.

SARA. Did you tell her that you were coming here?

LOT. No. I didn't think she would know. It is usually sundown before she wakens at this time of year. She doesn't stand the hot weather well.

SARA. [*Lightly*] One of these days, Lot, your wife's curiosity will be the death of her. [MILCAH *comes in.*] Good evening, Milcah. Come into the cool and rest. It is not like you to be abroad before the streets are in shadow.

MILCAH. I wondered where Lot had gone.

SARA. Hagar, a cool drink for Milcah. Lot, I am afraid I offered you nothing. A little wine?

LOT. Some whey, please.

MILCAH. Why should Lot go rushing out of the house into the heat?

LOT. I didn't rush.

MILCAH. If I hadn't happened to waken up I should never have known.

SARA. Would it have mattered?

MILCAH. It matters that one's husband should have secrets from one, surely.

LOT. There was no secret.

MILCAH. Then why did you not tell me that you were coming here?

LOT. It is not a matter of importance that I should visit my uncle's house.

MILCAH. Maybe not. But it is a sufficiently remarkable matter when you do it at an hour when you should be asleep at home.

SARA. [*Lightly*] Are you questioning my virtue, Milcah?

MILCAH. [*Impatient*] Of course not. What I am questioning is Lot's motive. He isn't borrowing money again, is he?

LOT. One would think that I was the only person since the Flood to borrow a little ready money.

SARA. It was not business that brought your husband through the hot streets, Milcah, my dear. It was sheer altruism. Wasn't it, Lot?

LOT. [*Not very comfortable under* SARA's *eye*] Of course it was.

SARA. He is worried about Abraham. [*Enter* HAGAR *with*

60

drink] Here is your cold drink, Milcah. [HAGAR *supplies the drinks and goes.*]

MILCAH. And can he not do his worrying under his own roof ? [*Taking her drink*] Thank you. I am as worried as he is——

SARA. You, too ?

MILCAH. No one likes having a relation who is rapidly becoming the talk of the town.

LOT. Oh, Milcah, you exaggerate. She always exaggerates.

MILCAH. Indeed I do not. My maid told me only yesterday that her brother's employer—he's a tanner in Eastgate—he told her brother that he had seen Abraham striding up the steps of the Ziggurat talking to himself and followed by five small boys making fun of him. It's a fine thing when one of the principal citizens of this town——

SARA. [*Hearing someone come into the house*] Hush ! [*They listen. ABRAHAM's voice can be heard in conversation with HAGAR*] That is Abraham now. Please don't mention these things to him. Whatever has led to his strangeness lately, I am sure that he is unaware of it. So don't suggest . . . Talk of other things. You have come for an evening visit. That is all. Talk of the Surveyor's new scheme. The drainage affair. Anything——

> *Enter ABRAHAM. He is no patriarch ; but a successful citizen of Ur. Handsome and well dressed. His voice is deep but quite gay. There is nothing high-falutin nor portentous about him.*

ABRAHAM. Hagar told me that we had guests. I am glad to see you, Lot. And you, Milcah. I hope you are both well. And I hope very much that you have not drunk everything that is cold in the house. [*Raising his voice*] Hagar ! [*As HAGAR answers, off, and comes running*] Some of that for me. How is business, Lot ?

LOT. Not bad for the time of year. Not bad at all.

SARA. [*Not accusing, merely rallying*] Whatever time of year it may be for business, it is the wrong time of year to be out-of-doors in the afternoon.

ABRAHAM. [*Mildly*] Yes. It was stupid of me. I forgot what time of day it was.

LOT. [*Unable to contain himself*] You forgot !

ABRAHAM. [*A little confused by the need of explanation*] Yes. I—I was thinking of other things.

MILCAH. One would have thought that the sun would have reminded you.

SARA. [*Sotto voce*] Milcah, *please!*

ABRAHAM. Yes. It's odd. I failed to notice the sun. [*As one making up his mind*] To be honest with you, things have been happening to me lately that I don't understand.

LOT. You're not worried about business, are you?

ABRAHAM. No, not at all. It is not a *worry* which dogs me. It is something much stranger. I am pursued by a Voice.

SARA. [*Gently*] A Voice?

ABRAHAM. A Voice that says: What are you doing here? What are you doing with your life in this city, where your days slip by as unremarkable as beads on a string? Is it for this you were born? To live the years round in the beauty and comfort of Ur until you go back to the dust of your beginning? Get up! Get out of this place, and see what there is for you elsewhere!

LOT. [*Half relieved*] But everyone feels like that in Ur at this time of year. There is not a man in the city but suffers from a weariness of the flesh and a desire to be elsewhere.

ABRAHAM. You think it is the season that troubles me? I could find it in my heart to wish that you were right. That my Voice was merely the breath of the hot wind. If that were so there would be respite to look forward to. As it is I am pursued by the Voice even in the first cool of the early morning. When the city is at its loveliest, and my desires can compass nothing more perfect than to be part of that beauty for the rest of my life. Even then the Voice is there. Urging me to go.

SARA. [*Still gently*] To go where, Abraham?

ABRAHAM. It doesn't say. All it says is that there is a great destiny for me elsewhere, and that I must leave Ur and follow it.

MILCAH. But that is absurd. It must be some kind of sickness. Have you consulted the priests? [*Enter* HAGAR *with drink.*

SARA. Hagar has brought your drink, dear. [*She prompts him gently, as one would a sick person or a child.*]

ABRAHAM. I don't wonder that you think that. I thought

62

that myself. For a whole winter and a spring I fought the Voice. I planned little ways to trick it. I invented new interests, designed new busynesses to fill my life, and said to myself : Now there will be no spare moment for the Voice. I have shut it out. I have defeated it. [*Wearily*] But it was no use. The Voice was everywhere.

SARA. Drink, my dear. You are tired.

ABRAHAM. Yes. Thank you. When the summer came it grew louder. It drowned the humming of the insects. It hammered at me when I walked through the street of the smiths. It talked, talked, talked among the palm leaves. It whispered in the dark as I lay sleepless at night.

LOT. *That* is what is wrong. These sleepless nights. No one sleeps well in this weather ; and lack of sleep does queer things to a man. Now, I know a first-class apothecary who can give you a draught that is as nearly a knock-out blow as makes no——

MILCAH. You and your apothecaries. I know a woman who will give him a charm, for half the money. A quite infallible charm. You tie it round your neck, and turn it over three times, say : " Thanks be to Nannar for night, and sleep, and the moon "—and you are asleep.

ABRAHAM. It is kind of you to suggest ; to want to help. But I shall need neither charm nor apothecary.

LOT. But you must have sleep or you will be really ill. And we can't afford to have you ill.

ABRAHAM. [*Calmly confident*] I shall sleep to-night.

LOT. How do you know ?

ABRAHAM. Because I have said " yes " to my destiny.

SARA. [*Puzzled*] What do you mean, Abraham ?

ABRAHAM. I would have told you after supper to-night. It happened to-day when I was walking on the highest terrace of the Ziggurat. In the town, when the Voice pursued me, I used to feel trapped. I used to hurry round street corners, and in and out of alleys, trying to escape. This was Ur, my city, and I didn't want to leave it. But to-day, from the high terrace, I could see the far distance ; like a promise. *That* was where my Voice bade me go and, once I could see it, it was not so frightening. Ur was, after all, only a small thing in a very wide world. And

63

somewhere in that world was the country of my destiny. " Go out," the Voice said, " and when you come into the country you will know it. To your children and your children's children I have given that country, and the whole world will be richer for it."

MILCAH. [*Scandalised*] " I " ! Who do you think the Voice is ?

ABRAHAM. [*As one having come to a conclusion*] I think it is God.

LOT. Which god ?

ABRAHAM. I don't know. This is the only one that has ever spoken to me. [*The sentence is unaccented. It is not " to me " nor " ever spoken." It is simple statement.*]

MILCAH. It is not the custom of the gods to speak except through a priest. It is much more likely to be a demon.

LOT. Milcah is right. It is not likely that a god would advise so strange a course. You had better consult the Temple authorities.

ABRAHAM. I have no need to consult anyone. [*Amending*] Any authority. [*He has remembered his wife*] Sara [*he sounds a little uncertain now*], you have said nothing.

SARA. What is there for me to say ? That I have faith in your Voice ? What faith can one have in a Voice whose promises are nonsense ?

ABRAHAM. Why should they be nonsense ?

SARA. The country is for your children's children, isn't it ? Have you forgotten that you are a childless man ?

ABRAHAM. [*Who has quite genuinely forgotten ; stubbornly*] The Voice says that it will be so ; and I believe it.

SARA. [*As it occurs to her for the first time*] It is possible, of course. It was stupid of me not to have seen it. You could . . . put me away and take another wife. A wife who——

ABRAHAM. [*Angrily*] I shall never have any wife but you. If my God gives me a country, he gives it to you too. And it is to your children that he will preserve it. [*He sounds almost as if he were giving notice.*]

SARA. Are you *bargaining* with your Voice ?

ABRAHAM. I believe what it says. I believe in my destiny ; and I have no destiny apart from you. When I go out from Ur you come with me ; and together we shall see the promise come true.

LOT. Leave Ur ! I think you must be insane. Where would you go ?

ABRAHAM. I don't know. I have not thought about it yet.

LOT. Where do you think there is a country for you to inherit ? Every square yard in all the thousand miles from Armenia to the sea, every inch that will grow a blade of grass, is the property of someone or other.

MILCAH. Perhaps he plans to live with the goats among the mountains.

ABRAHAM. No. I am no starving prophet. My inheritance is a rich one.

LOT. [*Pricking up his ears*] Rich ?

ABRAHAM. I have told you. There is a great future for me and for those belonging to me. Come with me, Lot, and share in it.

LOT. And what would I do with my business ? Make a gift of it to the priests ?

ABRAHAM. There is nothing in my Voice that says we must go out penniless. You could do what I am going to do. One share to the poor, one to the town, one to the Temple—I think they do some good [*he is not very sure about that but old habit is too much for him*]—and one in my purse.

MILCAH. Do you seriously mean that you are going to drag Sara away from all the people she knows, from all her friends, and the position she has made for herself in society, to go trailing round the world looking for a country that you don't even know the name of !

ABRAHAM. I am not dragging Sara anywhere. The promise is for her too. Everything I have ever had is Sara's. She knows that. This is hers too.

MILCAH. It is generous of you to give her something she doesn't want.

SARA. You mean well, Milcah, but I don't need you to defend me. This is between Abraham and me.

MILCAH. Well, we may as well go home and let you have it out with him. It will soon be supper-time anyhow.

LOT. I can't believe that you really mean to do this absurd, this fantastically ridiculous thing. I have always looked up to you as a shrewd and far-seeing man. It is incred——

ABRAHAM. And what makes you think that I have ceased to be far-seeing ? . . . [*As* LOT *hesitates at that—always afraid that he may miss something*] A view that embraces the whole earth and its possibilities can hardly be termed parochial. It is you, Lot, whose sight is short. I offer you a principality, but you prefer the security of a steady income in Ur.

MILCAH. [*Tartly*] You come home, Lot. You know very well that if you once begin to think you are missing something there is no folly that you are not capable of. [*To* ABRAHAM] Have you told anyone of your plans ? I mean, is there any reason why we shouldn't tell people ?

ABRAHAM. Until now I have never mentioned my Voice to anyone. No one, that is, except my father.

SARA. [*As one enlightened*] Ah !

LOT. Terah ! Don't tell me that you are thinking of taking Terah with you !

ABRAHAM. Of course. Why not ? Where I go, my father goes.

LOT. But the old man is an invalid—bedridden.

ABRAHAM. There are such things as litters. I shall never come back to Ur. I could hardly leave my father here to be attended by strangers.

MILCAH. But Lot and I could take him. That would be better for him than being jolted all over the Euphrates valley.

ABRAHAM. I have an idea that Lot may be coming with us.

MILCAH. Lot !

LOT. Not I ! Can you see me arranging my whole life at the bidding of a Voice ?

ABRAHAM. So far you have had to obey a great many voices. The voice of the priests—interpreting their god according to their fancy or the needs of the Temple. The voice of the King—ever changing as kings come and go. The voice of the Law—new and different with each new faculty. A hundred voices, competing, threatening, spelling confusion. I have finished with that. I have one Voice to obey. And what I do is between me and my God.

MILCAH. [*With decision*] Lot, come home.

SARA. [*With the pressing claims of hospitality*] We can give you supper. It is onion soup, and cold meat with cucumber.

MILCAH. Thank you, but I know that you want to talk to Abraham. And anyhow, Lot shouldn't have cucumber.

SARA. They are just garnish. He doesn't have to eat it.

MILCAH. If there are cucumbers there, Lot will eat them. I am sorry that I came so unceremoniously. I didn't know that you were in trouble. I was angry because Lot had sneaked out without telling me. Good night. I shall get my " charm " woman to give me something to alter Abraham's mind. It is wonderful what she can do with a few bits and pieces. So perhaps it will all blow over. But if it doesn't, remember that we will be happy to look after old Terah. I like the old man. He was the first to say a kind word to me when I came into this family. And of course Lot is terrified of him, which is very useful. [*Only part of this speech is audible to* LOT, *who is busy with* ABRAHAM] Are you ready, Lot ?

LOT. Yes, I'm coming. Good night, Aunt Sara—and my sympathy.

SARA. Good night to you both. Good night.

They go. There is a short pause.

ABRAHAM. She said : You will want to talk to Abraham.

SARA. [*Avoiding the main point*] Would it not have helped you to *tell* me about the Voice ? Were you so little sure of me ?

ABRAHAM. If I could not believe, myself, how could I expect belief from you ?

SARA. It was not belief I meant, but sympathy in your trouble.

ABRAHAM. [*Quickly*] But you believe now ! You believe that my Voice is a true and good thing ?

SARA. [*Slowly*] I believe that you have to leave Ur.

ABRAHAM. You think that I am possessed.

SARA. I think you cannot help yourself.

ABRAHAM. In other words, I am a madman. And what has sent me mad, do you think ?

SARA. I don't know. Does it matter ?

ABRAHAM. Matter ?

SARA. Mad or sane, you are Abraham, and my husband. And

I will go with you out of Ur to-morrow morning if that is what you want.

ABRAHAM. [*His resentment of her disbelief melting into something like wistfulness*] I wish you believed.

SARA. [*Gently reproving*] It is a little greedy of you to want belief *too*.

ABRAHAM. [*Following his own thought*] If I had told you to-night, as I planned, when we were alone, you might have believed.

SARA. No one who has not heard your Voice for himself could believe, Abraham. You must see that. Did Terah believe when you told him ?

ABRAHAM. [*Thoughtfully, seeing her point*] No. No, I suppose he didn't. He just listened. [*Remembering something*] Why did you say " Ah ! " when I said that I had told Terah about the Voice ?

SARA. Because then I knew why the old man had looked with pity at me when I gave him his broth this morning.

ABRAHAM. Pity ? Why should he pity you ?

SARA. Because he knew that I would have no defence against you.

ABRAHAM. Defence ?

SARA. We will follow you out of Ur, Terah and I, because we love you. We have no ear for your Voice, but your way is our way, and your God our God. [*Putting out her hand to him, matter of fact, gently*] Come to supper.

CURTAIN

MRS. FRY HAS A VISITOR

CHARACTERS

In order of appearance

YOUNG LADY.   MRS. FRY.

*A room in a London suburban house in the early forties of last
century. In a wheeled chair is sitting an impressive old lady
in Quaker attire. A book is lying on her lap and spectacles are
still on her nose, but she is not reading. Her eyes are closed,
and her face, until lately so confident, so energetic, so—shall
we say it?—domineering, has slipped into lines of sadness,
weakness, and doubt.*

*There is a tentative tap on the door, of which the dreaming old
woman seems to be unaware, and the door opens to admit a
charming and fashionable YOUNG LADY. She is in her early
twenties, and has a gentle and composed manner, tinged now
with shyness since she is evidently a stranger in the room. She
closes the door quietly, and stands for a moment looking across
the room at her hostess.*

YOUNG LADY. [*Tentatively*] Mrs. Fry. [MRS. FRY *opens her
eyes, puts up a slow arm to remove her glasses, and turns her head to
look*] Your maid said that I might come in.

MRS. FRY. Oh, yes. Come in, my dear. You wanted to speak
to me.

Y. L. [*Advancing into the room*] It is very kind of you to see
me—a stranger. Especially when you are ill.

MRS. FRY. [*Dryly*] You have been listening to Mary. I am
not ill. Merely an old woman—and a little sad.

Y. L. Sad, Mrs. Fry ?

MRS. FRY. Find a chair, my dear. [*The* YOUNG LADY *is too
much interested in* MRS. FRY *to withdraw her attention, and presently
she sinks on the stool by* MRS. FRY'S *chair*] It is always a sad thing
to come to the end of one's life before one has come to the end of
one's work.

Y. L. But, Mrs. Fry, there will always be someone to carry on your work. Women who will devote themselves to it heart and soul, as you have.

MRS. FRY. They say that queens are apt to look with a bleak eye on their successors. I can understand their emotions. Even a cook finds it difficult to believe that anyone can roast a chicken as well as she can. How much more when a woman has changed the face of humanity does she . . . But it is vanity, of course, and very reprehensible. I pray constantly for humility. Don't sit on the stool, child. There is a comfortable chair over there.

Y. L. [*Not moving*] It was to sit at your feet that I came. You must think it very presumptuous of me to force myself on you like this. But I had wanted to see you for a very long time. I kept hoping that we might meet somewhere. By accident, I mean. That I might walk into some drawing-room and find you there. In fact, it was the only thing that made paying calls with Mamma bearable. I used to say to myself : Perhaps, who knows, Mrs. Fry will be there. And when you were not : Oh, well, perhaps to-morrow at the Bracebridges, or the day after at the Herberts. It gave some meaning to the silly business. And then I heard that you were not going out any more. And so I made up my mind to come to see you. It took me some weeks to get up my courage—and I must confess when I was confronted with your maid my courage dropped quite a lot.

MRS. FRY. [*Amused*] Yes, Mary is very formidable. Even I quaver occasionally before Mary. [*Looking on her visitor with a new eye*] It occurs to me that if you overcame Mary you must . . . [*She is going to say : " You must be something more than a silly and fashionable young woman " but she thinks better of it*] Did you come alone ?

Y. L. No, I confided in Aunt Mai, and she brought me in the carriage. She is driving round until I come out. We are supposed to be buying stockings.

MRS. FRY. Am I to understand that I would be considered a bad influence ?

Y. L. Oh, no. No, of course not. But you *would* be held to be . . . adding fuel to my oddity, so to speak.

MRS. FRY. Are you odd ?

Y. L. According to my family, I am extremely odd. You see, the life they lead seems to me quite ridiculous. A waste of time, and energy, and interest. I am bored to desperation by their activities.

MRS. FRY. What is wrong with this family of yours? Is it not a pleasant and united one?

Y. L. United, Mrs. Fry, is the appropriate word. Every evening we sit united in the drawing-room and watch the hands of the clock move round to ten, when we retire. Every morning Papa reads *The Times* aloud to my sister and me. It takes hours. Parthe—that's my sister—Parthe goes on with her drawing, but for me—for me it is like lying on one's back with one's hands tied and having liquid poured down one's throat. I don't know which is worse: those endless evenings or those boring mornings. In the afternoon we receive, or pay calls. All my life I have wanted to do useful things; big, important things; and what have I done this last fortnight? I have read the *Daughter at Home* to Papa; a volume of *Sybil* to Mamma. Learned seven tunes by heart. Paid eight visits. And written a few letters.

MRS. FRY. Those " useful " things you talk about . . . [*She pauses in question.*]

Y. L. I want to do work like yours. You went into the prisons when no woman would dream of doing such a thing. I expect they thought that *you* were very odd. And you made those dreadful sties into clean, healthy places. That is done, but there are so many other things crying to be done; so many. I have tried to help the poor in the villages——

MRS. FRY. [*Interrupting*] The villages?

Y. L. Papa has two country places; one in Derbyshire and one in the New Forest. I look after the sick people in the villages, and try to improve their condition, to teach them things—or as much as I know myself. My family let me do that, because it is a ladylike enough occupation, and they are our own people. But when I suggest that I might go somewhere and learn a little myself—to a hospital or some such place—they are horrified. What am I to do, Mrs. Fry? The precious days run away to waste. What am I to do?

MRS. FRY. Tell me, child : you are very young and attractive ; have you no suitors ?

Y. L. Oh, yes ; I have the usual amount.

MRS. FRY. And you are not drawn to any of them ?

Y. L. There is one whom I find pleasant. [*Dropping the subject*] But I don't want to marry anyone. I don't want to spend my life in domestic duties ; in ordering meals and seeing that the dusting is done. I want to devote my life to serving the community.

MRS. FRY. Marriage, my dear, is even more indispensable to the community than hospitals. [*As her visitor is about to interrupt*] There may be nothing very glorious in making a home ; but anything and everything may be done to the glory of God.

Y. L. [*In a burst*] Mrs. Fry, I will *not* spend my life arranging flowers to the glory of God. [*More quietly ; half apologetic for her bluntness, half accusing*] I thought that you would understand ; you of all people.

MRS. FRY. You must not think me unsympathetic because I show you other roads. You come to me for comfort ; for advice, perhaps. I have to think, then, of *your* happiness as well as the needs of the poor. I should not like you to miss the happiness that marriage can bring. I have brought up a large family, and I can . . . [*she falters a moment*] can compare the relative values of children's love and of—of . . . [*Her voice dies away and she appears to be musing.*]

Y. L. [*Gently*] Mrs. Fry, I *know* where my happiness lies. What I don't know is how to achieve it. I thought that you might help me. That you might tell me how *you* managed your family—when you were a girl, I mean, and your mind was filled with thoughts of service for others.

MRS. FRY. [*Dreamily*] My mind was filled with nothing but a pair of boots.

Y. L. Boots !

MRS. FRY. How strange. I had not remembered those boots for fifty years. Purple, they were ; with scarlet laces. Very smart. I went to Meeting in them, and thought a great deal more about them than I did about God. A very frivolous young creature I was; with an eighteen-inch waist and a liking for military bands. And then, when I was admiring my boots, I suddenly heard what the preacher was saying; and I found it so moving that I cried. I went home and shed my finery and became a " plain Friend ". [*She pauses and resumes in a drier tone*] I became, too, a great affliction to my sisters. The worst of virtue is its tendency to self-righteousness. Are you an affliction to your family, do you think ?

Y. L. [*Startled by this new viewpoint*] I don't know. I had not thought of it. I *hope* I am.

MRS. FRY. [*Startled in her turn*] You hope so ?

Y. L. If I afflict them sufficiently they may be moved to let me go. Like Pharaoh after the plagues.

MRS. FRY. [*Smiling at her*] My dear, you are much too charming to turn yourself into a plague. Why not go on with your good work in the villages, and find your happiness there.

Y. L. Because I don't know enough ! I must learn. I must fit myself for my work. I will *not* be an amateur ; a ladylike dabbler in lotions ; a district visitor with cake and calf's-foot jelly in a basket. I want to do serious work.

MRS. FRY. But in your own villages there is scope, surely, for——

Y. L. [*Breaking in*] Oh, Mrs. Fry, *why* do you discourage me ! [*It is a* cri de cœur.]

MRS. FRY. [*Mildly*] Because, my child, in the course of my long life a great many fashionable young ladies have come to me, filled with visions of service, of self-sacrifice. They all had excellent hearts, but no sense of reality. They saw themselves leading a crusade, with banners flying. Now, the essence of crusading is not banners, but remembering to pack the spoons. And not one of these young women was a spoon-packer.

Y. L. But I am not like that. I am the most practical person in the world. You think because I wear expensive clothes that I am a ninny. But that is not fair. It is not my fault that Papa is well-to-do, and that I was brought up to be ornamental, and sent abroad to be finished, and presented at Court, and dragged round in a carriage as if I had lost the use of my legs. I am not to be blamed for that. Am I not doing my best to escape from such an existence ? Was it not to look for help in such an escape that I came here this afternoon ?

MRS. FRY. [*Smiling a little ; kindly*] And now you are beginning to be sorry you came.

Y. L. Oh, no. However much you snub me, you are still Elizabeth Fry and I have met and talked to you. That is a great thing. But . . .

MRS. FRY. But what ?

Y. L. If you will forgive my being frank, you puzzle me.

MRS. FRY. In what way ?

Y. L. Well, for one thing, you too came from a leisured home. I have read everything that has been written about you, you see. And that has not prevented your being efficient and practical. Why should you take it for granted that—that . . .

MRS. FRY. [*Supplying the words*] That I am unique.

Y. L. [*Accepting this*] It is almost as if you didn't *want* me to do the work ; as if you did not approve of the idea. You—you sound almost like Mamma.

MRS. FRY. I take it that that is the height of opprobrium. [*As her visitor is about to amend her speech*] No, don't alter it, my child. I like frankness. Would it shock you if I said that I did *not* approve ?

Y. L. [*At a loss*] I don't think I should believe it. Why *should* you disapprove ? It can't be merely because you want me to please my parents.

MRS. FRY. No. I did not please mine.

Y. L. Nor because you think the work is unwomanly or some such thing.

MRS. FRY. No ; it is a woman's work.

Y. L. Then why ?

MRS. FRY. Because I like you, my dear, and I want you to be happy. And public service gives great rewards, but happiness, earthly or spiritual, is not one of them.

Y. L. [*After a pause of astonishment*] But, Mrs. Fry, I can imagine no greater happiness on earth than to have achieved what you have. To have bettered the lot of thousands of human beings. There *can* be no greater happiness.

74

Mrs. Fry. It is a satisfaction, of course. A greater satisfaction would be one's children's love.

Y. L. But . . . [*She cannot venture into speech.*]

Mrs. Fry. [*Understanding what she would have said*] Oh, yes ;
they are devoted to me. They are good children. But in their
hearts they think of me as Elizabeth Fry. Elizabeth Fry, the
darling of the committees. It is not a very *cosy* thing to have a
mother who is a detachable part of a committee. And power,
my child, is a corrupting thing. A veritable cancer of the spirit.
One continually wants more of it. Soon the praise begins to
sound sweet in one's ears. One develops an appetite for it. One
begins to accept oneself at the world's valuation. And what is
left then ? Nothing but a monstrous image, as false and hollow
as the horse of Troy. [*She pauses ; and then in a brisker, conversational tone*] And if you think, my dear young lady, that
nothing in the least like that would ever happen to you,
you are greatly wrong. That is exactly what happens to every
one who is given worldly power. Since I have been ill I have
had time to look back on my life. [*Returning to contemplation
again*] What a very vain, domineering creature I turned out
to be.

Y. L. That I can *not* believe.

Mrs. Fry. [*Her mind busy with the past*] I had a beautiful
voice when I was young. Everyone remarked upon it ; and I
read aloud to the general admiration. The admiration was so
general that I read aloud to all and sundry for fifty years. Men,
women, and children ; the sick, the heartbroken, the illiterate ;
they were moved to the point of tears. And then, just lately, I
fell ill, and *I* was read aloud to. And believe me, my child, I
know now why those unhappy people wept.

Y. L. [*Amused*] I confess that it is not one of my favourite
amusements. But, Mrs. Fry, everyone has a small vanity ; that
they——

Mrs. Fry. No vanity is small. It is the drop which poisons
the whole. At the very moment when I was praying God for
humility my mind would present me with the fact that the
Duchess of Gloucester was coming to dine.

Y. L. But that is not vanity ! It is no more vanity than

noticing the pattern of the carpet. It can never have mattered to you that royalty should pay you attention.

MRS. FRY. [*Considering it*] No. [*Dryly*] But one began to notice it if they failed to.

Y. L. [*Desperate and putting her hand down*] Mrs. Fry, if you went to bed every night with Debrett, it wouldn't alter the fact that old Mrs. Vigor has a bad leg and that the greatest ambition of my life is to make it a good one. You bother me with abstractions, and all I care about is brass tacks. First you hold up the theoretical joys of marriage——

MRS. FRY. [*Horrified*] My dear young lady !

Y. L. Then you suggest that I am impractical. Then you prophesy that I should become a monster of vanity. *Please*, Mrs. Fry, let us talk about *bad legs*. Bad legs and how I can cure them.

MRS. FRY. [*Not much liking the turn in the conversation*] The first duty of a good nurse, I have always understood, is to obey the doctor's orders.

Y. L. Which doctor ? Old Mrs. Vigor has had seven. They all prescribed different things. And she still has her bad leg.

MRS. FRY. That suggests to me that the leg is incurable.

Y. L. What it suggests to me is that the doctors don't know their business.

MRS. FRY. Is not that a little presumptuous in a young, untrained——

Y. L. [*Interrupting*] If I could go somewhere and *learn*. See a great many sick people, and see what is done for them. What is tried and what fails. I know I could cure old Mrs. Vigor.

MRS. FRY. Do you consider yourself wiser than a doctor ?

Y. L. I don't know about wiser. I *wash* a great deal oftener. And I can bandage a great deal better. And I don't think that because a thing was laid down in the year 500 it is necessarily either truth or wisdom. And I don't consider that I am omniscient and beyond criticism. I don't believe myself to be an oracle.

MRS. FRY. [*With gentle malice*] Don't you, my dear ?

Y. L. [*Brought up with a round turn ; humour breaking through*] Oh, Mrs. Fry ! Is that what I sound like ?

MRS. FRY. I think you are well on the *way* to being an oracle.

Y. L. [*Contemplating it*] How dreadful if all I turned out to be was a dragon. [*Taking heart*] Well, I wouldn't mind even that if I dragooned people into being well. They could curse me all they liked as long as they stood up on their own two feet to do it. I can imagine no lovelier moment than . . . [*She pauses to listen*] I think I hear . . . That sounds like the carriage. [*Going to the window*] Oh, yes, it is! It's Aunt Mai, back already. Oh, dear, now I shall have to go. And I have said none of the things . . . I haven't even convinced you . . . I have intruded and bothered you all to no purpose. You don't believe in me. You think I am a romantic-minded ninny. You——

MRS. FRY. [*Soothing, but unconvincing*] No, my dear, no.

Y. L. You have held up one bogy after another to frighten and dissuade me. You——

MRS. FRY. No, my child, no. I think you are a very fine young woman with an excellent heart and great vitality. [*She is quite unconsciously patronising; like most women who have become legends in their own day she finds it difficult to believe that her quality can be duplicated.*]

Y. L. That means I am restless.

MRS. FRY. [*Still gently patronising*] A little headstrong, perhaps. Like all young things. But willing to serve others; and that is a great thing. Learn to harness that willingness to an appropriate object. Be content with your own small corner of usefulness. You will find it rewarding. Go on with your good work in the villages, my dear. And some day I hope you will marry that suitor whom you "find pleasant"; and that you will bring your first child to see me if I am still here.

Y. L. It was kind of you to see *me*, to-day. I shall always be grateful to you for that—even if you don't believe in me. I know it was presumptuous of me to invade your privacy, to force myself upon you. A great many importunate people must have—must have attacked that privacy at one time or another. It was kind of you to listen to one more. Forgive me for tiring you, won't you?

MRS. FRY. [*Refusing the suggestion of tiredness*] No, it has been pleasant to talk with a young creature, and remember my own youth.

Y. L. I must go now. Aunt Mai will be waiting.

MRS. FRY. Goodbye, my dear. [*She sounds a little distrait.*]

Y. L. Goodbye, Mrs. Fry ; and thank you again.

MRS. FRY. [*As the* YOUNG LADY *reaches the door ; without emphasis or great interest*] Mary told me your name, but I forget what she said.

Y. L. Nightingale, Mrs. Fry. Florence Nightingale.

MRS. FRY *nods her acknowledgment and picks up her spectacles.*

CURTAIN

THREE MRS. MADDERLEYS

CHARACTERS

In order of appearance

MARY.	WAITER.
MARGOT.	MARION.

The scene is the terrace of a hotel in a fashionable holiday resort. At one of the little iron tables set among the potted shrubs is MARY MADDERLEY. *She is going to be forty-one next month, and has never attempted to conceal the fact. Her rather long, kind face is innocent of make-up. Her features, like her clothes, are good; but both lack verve. Her manner is tinged with shyness, and there is an odd suggestion of immaturity about her; as of one who has always lived dependent on another. On the table in front of her is a half-drunk glass of pale sherry.*
Along the terrace comes MARGOT MADDERLEY. *She is twenty. Self-confident, fashionable, very pretty. She has a bored expression and a faintly hard-boiled air; but neither is native to her. The boredom was merely "the thing" in the senior forms at her very expensive school; and the hard-boiled air was "the thing" with her set in the years since she left school. She is being pursued along the terrace, although she doesn't know it, by a waiter clutching a library book. She sits down at the table next to* MARY'S, *and begins a hunt through her bag for a lighter.*

MARY. [*Tentatively*] If it is matches you are looking for, there are some here on my table. [*Her voice is sweet and immature.*]

MARGOT. [*In a bored contralto drawl*] Yes. My damned lighter's lost again.

WAITER. [*Coming up, breathless*] Madame Madderley? Madame left her book in the foyer. I thought Madame might miss it. [*He has the air of a puppy retrieving a stick; proud and willing.*]

79

MARGOT. [*Receiving it without enthusiasm*] Oh. Thanks. Bring me a pink gin, will you.

WAITER. At once, madame. [*He goes.*]

MARGOT. [*Busy with her cigarette-lighting*] Might as well be a convict.

MARY. [*Startled*] A convict?

MARGOT. As go about with a library book. Name and number indelibly fixed.

MARY. [*Smiling a little*] Oh. I see. Yes; Cash's used to give me the same feeling.

MARGOT. [*Looking at her for the first time*] Cash's?

MARY. Those names in tape on one's school clothes. One was labelled down to the very combinations.

MARGOT. Never wore the things. [*Relenting*] But I remember Cash's.

MARY. [*Looking at her kindly*] I should hope so. [*In answer to* MARGOT'S *enquiring glance*] It can't be very long since you stopped wearing school things.

MARGOT. Between five and six thousand years.

MARY. [*Smiling at her a little*] You wear remarkably well. [*As this produces a more or less friendly glance from* MARGOT] Forgive me, but I think I heard the waiter call you Madderley. That's odd, because it is not a very common name, and it happens to be mine too. [*She is not being in the least curious; merely friendly.*]

MARGOT. [*Not interested*] Really? Well, it won't be mine for very long.

MARY. Oh? You are going to be married?

MARGOT. No. Divorced.

MARY. Oh; I am sorry.

MARGOT. Don't be. It is what is known as a happy release. [MARY *makes a small cooing noise of sympathy.*] I made a horrible mistake. I married for love.

MARY. But surely that is the proper thing to marry for!

MARGOT. Next time, I promise you, I shall be highly improper. [*Glancing at the ring on* MARY'S *hand*] I see that you wear a ring. Did you marry for love?

MARY. [*Warmly*] Oh, yes.

MARGOT. And did it work ?

MARY. For twenty years it did.

MARGOT. And then ?

MARY. He fell in love with someone else. [*After a slight pause*] Is . . . that what has happened to you ?

MARGOT. Oh, no. He dotes upon me. At least, he did until last night.

MARY. Last night ? [*Relieved*] Oh, you mean you have just had a quarrel, and that all this talk of divorce——

MARGOT. [*Incisively*] Last night is when he will have had my lawyer's letter.

MARY. [*Dashed*] Oh.

MARGOT. [*Pleased*] It will be a shock to him.

MARY. Yes, I expect so.

MARGOT. He sees himself as a combination of King Arthur and Gabriel. The Archangel Gabriel. The letter is to say he is a poor fish, a crashing bore, and plain poison. Wrapped up legally, of course, but he will get the general idea.

MARY. Dear me. How long have you lived with this . . . horror ?

MARGOT. Eighteen months. Seventeen months and twenty-nine days too long. But I was romantic about him. He *looks* a little like Gabriel, you see. Stern, and beautiful, and the perfect gent.

MARY. [*A far-away look in her eyes*] Ah, yes.

MARGOT. You recognise the type ?

MARY. Yes.

MARGOT. [*Examining her with more interest*] You are still in love with your husband, aren't you ?

MARY. [*Matter-of-fact*] Oh, yes. One doesn't fall out of love just because the other one does, you know. That is why I can't help being a little sorry for your poor archangel. If he loves you so much, he is not likely to be cured by a lawyer's letter.

MARGOT. John has never been in love with anyone but himself.

MARY. [*Her attention wholly arrested*] John ?

MARGOT. He dotes on me just as he dotes on his old sherry, and his new golf clubs, and his old Spode.

MARY. [*Her worst fears confirmed*] Spode !

MARGOT. Yes; china, you know. He *collected* me, along with the other things. Ah, here is my drink!

WAITER. [*Coming up with a tray*] One pink gin for madame.

MARY. [*In a faint voice*] I think *I* should like one of those.

MARGOT. You haven't finished your sherry. Is it revolting?

MARY. No; but I think I could do with one of these.

WAITER. At once, madame.

MARY. I shall finish the sherry while you are bringing it.

WAITER. Very good, madame. [*He goes.*]

MARGOT. [*Taking her first sip, with satisfaction*] John didn't approve of pink gins.

MARY. [*Unguardedly*] No.

MARGOT. How do you mean, no?

MARY. [*Retrieving hastily*] I mean, the Gabriel type don't, do they?

MARGOT. No. That is one of the flaws I had as a collector's piece. He was always pointing out my flaws. [MARY'S *ears prick a little, as if that had a familiar sound.*] I was quite worried about them until I got wise to him.

MARY. Until you . . . ?

MARGOT. Until the halo dropped off.

MARY. [*Faintly*] Did that take long?

MARGOT. It began to slip towards the end of the second month. By the sixth it had gone. There was a tiny bald spot there instead. I told him about the bald spot, but he was furious and went and spent the night at Marion's.

MARY. Marion.

MARGOT. Marion is John's mother. He said it was to talk about her investments, but it was just because of the bald spot. His mental age is five and a half.

MARY. [*Half fascinated, half repudiating*] But he is a . . . He is very good at his profession, surely?

MARGOT. [*In a that-proves-nothing tone*] Oh, yes. A great many *lunatics* are *mathematical geniuses*. What a man does in an office is no guide to what he is capable of doing outside it.

MARY. No; no, I suppose not.

MARGOT. It was a shock to find I had married someone aged five and a half.

MARY. Yes. Yes, I suppose it must.

MARGOT. Especially when he is forty-two and looks like Gabriel.

MARY. But . . . [*She looks round for some defence of John.*]

MARGOT. But what ?

MARY. But surely he has—has qualities; great charm, perhaps ?

MARGOT. He has so much charm that it drips off him. After a little you don't notice anything but the pool on the floor.

MARY. And is he not faithful ? And honest ?

MARGOT. Oh, yes. He also washes behind his ears.

MARY. [*Giving it up*] I am sorry you couldn't make it a success. You are so young and—and vivid. John is bound to miss you frightfully.

MARGOT. [*Equally*] Oh, no. He has Mary.

MARY. [*Electrified*] Mary !

MARGOT. His first wife. We lived with Mary.

MARY. But—but how could you ?

MARGOT. I couldn't. Mary licked me.

MARY. I don't understand.

MARGOT. Mary was perfect. There was nothing I did from morning till night but Mary had done it better. The only way I was Mary's successor was chronologically. No one arranged flowers like Mary, no one wore clothes like Mary, no one knew how to cure his colds in the head like Mary—and my God, what colds ! No one was ever so wise, so kind, so lovely, so intelligent as Mary. Living with John was a bore, but living with Mary was unbearable. I never saw the woman, but if she suffered John for twenty years and still kept his admiration she must have either the soul of a saint or the hide of a rhinoceros. I wish that man would come with your drink. I want another. [*Considering* MARY] You know, I wouldn't have said that gin was your tipple.

MARY. It isn't, usually.

MARGOT. I hope my matrimonial infelicities haven't brought yours to the surface again.

MARY. I'm afraid they have, rather. You see, I'm Mary.

MARGOT. [*Caught off-balance for once*] *You* are ! [*Considering her anew*] Well ! [*Recovering her poise*] That makes John a liar as well as a poor fish.

MARY. John ?

MARGOT. He said you dressed better than any woman he ever knew.

MARY. [*Humbly*] No, I'm afraid I never took much interest in clothes. [*Looking at* MARGOT *with simple admiration*] They told me you were pretty. [*The emphasis is on "told"; she is merely confirming the fact.*]

MARGOT. [*Drawling*] Thanks. All my own work. Why don't *you* give chemistry a chance ?

MARY. [*At a loss*] I don't under——

MARGOT. You are much better looking than I am. I know John said you were very economical——

MARY. He said *that* !

MARGOT. —but five pounds spent in the right places and you would be a raving beauty.

MARY. I suppose it's dreadful of me, but I would rather have the five pounds.

MARGOT. Didn't you do anything to keep John ? I mean, when he began to slip.

MARY. It wasn't a slip ; it was a landslide. He just came home one day and told me that he had fallen in love with someone else.

MARGOT. I can see him. Very grave, and frank, and noble.

MARY. There wasn't much I could do about it, was there ?

MARGOT. You could have shot me, but I suppose it didn't occur to you.

MARY. No. I just hoped that you would make him happy.

MARGOT. [*In simple comment*] My God ! [*Cheerfully*] Well, now I know why providence kept me from murdering John.

MARY. Why ?

MARGOT. So that you could have him back intact.

MARY. [*Sweetly and mildly*] But I don't want him back.

MARGOT. [*Staggered for once*] You don't !

MARY. No ; I have only just this moment got free of him.

MARGOT. But a minute ago you told me you were still in love with him.

MARY. That was before I heard about all my charming qualities.

MARGOT. What has that to——

MARY. You see, I lived with someone too. Only the person I lived with was my mother-in-law.

MARGOT. Marion.

MARY. Yes.

MARGOT. Not actually ?

MARY. No, the way you lived with me. For twenty years I tried to be like Marion. John adored his mother, and I tried not to be a—an anti-climax. But it was difficult. What was it you said : " No one was ever so wise, so kind, so intelligent, so lovely "— as Marion. No one wore clothes like Marion, arranged flowers like Marion—and so on and so on and so on.

MARGOT. Well, I'll be . . . !

MARY. Marion *is* rather wonderful, of course. So I didn't mind trying to live up to her.

MARGOT. Didn't mind !

MARY. Not actively. I was very humble about myself. After twenty years I was a little tired but still humble, and still trying. When John fell in love with you I took it that I had failed.

MARGOT. And your heart broke.

MARY. My heart cracked wide open. It mended with a click five minutes ago. To be exact, on the word " economical ". You're sure John told you I was economical ?

MARGOT. Every time a bill came in. Are you not ?

MARY. For twenty years he told me daily what a bad manager I was. He was very sweet about it ; very patient ; always hoping I would do better next time.

MARGOT. [*Contemplating it*] You know, all we've been, you and I, is a couple of donkeys with carrots dangled in front of our noses.

MARY. With a difference. [*In answer to* MARGOT'S *eyebrows*] I ran after my carrot.

MARGOT. You certainly ran.

MARY. You mustn't blame me too much. Marion brought him up to expect perfection. Do you know her ?

MARGOT. [*Extra sec*] We have met. A strong-minded woman.

MARY. Yes. John was stamped in her image before we met. It seemed natural to conform to the mould. She rarely came to see us, and yet she pervaded the house.

MARGOT. You practically stank the place out when I lived there.

MARY. [*With a laughing expulsion of her breath*] I even came to this place because she used to talk about it. Her sister is married to a clergyman here. Ah, here is the waiter.

WAITER. One pink gin for madame.

MARGOT. O—h, no! We have changed all that. You take that away and bring us a bottle of champagne.

MARY. But I would like to have the gin. I've never had one, you know.

MARGOT. Gin may be good for drowning one's sorrows in, but it is no drink for a celebration. You bring us some Pol Roger, waiter. The best vintage year you have.

WAITER. At once, Madame.

MARY. Very well. But I insist on tasting a pink gin, so you may leave it, waiter.

WAITER. Very good, madame. [*He goes.*]

MARY. John, as you remarked, didn't approve of gin. [*She embarks on her drink with an air of having at last achieved equality with John.*]

MARGOT. My blessing on your emancipation.

MARY. It tastes rather like wood shavings.

MARGOT. It gets better as you go on.

MARY. Poor darling John.

MARGOT. Hurrah!

MARY. Why?

MARGOT. You have reached the stage of patronising him.

MARY. I was thinking of the shock that lawyer's letter would be to him.

MARGOT. You were not. You were thinking how nice it was that he was going to be shocked.

MARY. Was I? Perhaps I was. How malicious of me. Oh, well; Marion will be there to hold his hand.

MARGOT. As it happens, she won't.

MARY. No? Why?

MARGOT. Because she is coming down the path from the annexe at this moment.

MARY. Marion is! *This* path?

MARGOT. In her black-and-white foulard and her garden-party hat. Good God, don't drink gin in a gulp like that! [*Raising her voice to greet* MARION *as she approaches*] Hello, there.

> MARION *is a good-looking woman; tall, grey, slender, with a pleasant voice and a firm, composed manner. Her clothes are in excellent taste, and they are worn much better than* MARY'S *are.*

MARION. Margot! My dear child! What are you doing here?

MARGOT. Waiting for a drink.

MARION. And Mary too! How nice. And how very surprising.

MARGOT. Will you have this chair. The champagne won't be long.

MARION. Champagne! You extravagant hussies. Are you celebrating something?

MARY. We are about to celebrate our coming of age.

MARION. My darling Mary, you sound as if you had been celebrating already. Where is John?

MARGOT. It being ten and one-half minutes to one o'clock, John is at this moment descending the second flight of stairs at the office on his way to lunch.

MARION. You mean that John is not here?

MARGOT. Not even in spirit.

MARY. Poor John. [*She gives a sudden little giggle.*]

MARION. Mary, my dear! [*Glancing at* MARY'S *drink; quite uncensorious*] Is that gin?

MARY. It's a *pink* gin.

MARION. Is that a good introduction to champagne, do you think? And anyhow, why "poor John"?

MARGOT. She is sorry for John because I have left him.

MARION. Left him? Behind? Or for good?

MARGOT. Both. [*Genuine*] I'm sorry if it distresses you.

MARION. [*Slowly*] I regret it, of course. It is a pity. But I must confess that from some points of view it may be an excellent thing.

MARGOT. [*Aggressive; taking it for granted that* MARION *thinks that she is good riddance*] You do!

MARION. Don't think me harsh, my dear—I'm devoted to John, you know—but I can't help thinking that—well, that he was becoming just the least little bit in the world *smug.*

MARY. [*Into the astonished pause*] Marion, you surprise me.

MARGOT. She *staggers* me.

MARION. Why ?

MARGOT. One hadn't expected you to be critical of John. After all, he is your creation.

MARION. Only physically. The rest is Nannie's.

MARY. Nannie ?

MARION. You didn't know Nannie. She was my mother's old nurse. A strong-minded woman. [*This is what* MARGOT *has said of her, although she does not know it.*] I, being a young widow with a profession to occupy me, had to leave John to Nannie. I may as well confess to you that I was inordinately jealous of Nannie. She always did everything better than I did.

MARGOT. [*Her attention arrested*] She *what* ?

MARION. [*Misunderstanding her emphasis*] I mean, things for John. Domestic things.

MARGOT. For instance ?

MARION. Oh . . . [*she looks round for samples*] if I bought him woollies they were too thick and scratched ; if I told him stories at night Nannie had told him better ones ; if I took him for a walk it wasn't as exciting as Nannie's, because Nannie's walks had ponds in them, and fish, and what not . . . [*With the breath of a rueful laugh*] I spent the best years of my life trying to live up to Nannie.

MARGOT. [*In great delight*] MARY ! She had a carrot too !

MARION. A *what* ?

MARY. [*Happily ; making a sing-song chant of it*] No one told stories like Nannie, no one arranged flowers like Nannie, no one wore clothes like Nannie, no one was ever so wise, so kind, so intelligent, so lovely——

MARION. Mary, my dear, you *are* drunk. You are behaving very strangely, you two.

MARGOT. You tell her, Mary. You're a graduate.

MARION. What *is* all this, Mary ?

MARY. Marion, I hate to tell you, but you are a donkey.

MARION. Margot, you appear to be sober. Will you tell me.

MARGOT. It's not gin that Mary's drunk with, but relief.

MARION. Relief from what ?

MARGOT. John. She has just discovered that he is a black-mailer.

MARION. Margot, do stop this absurdity, and tell me . . .

MARGOT. Remember the way he used to hold Nannie over your head ?

MARION. I don't know that I should put it that way exactly. [*But her tone is doubtful ; that is just what he used to do.*]

MARGOT. He dug a lot of extras out of you with Nannie for a lever, didn't he. [*It is statement, not question.*]

MARION. You don't put it very elegantly, my dear, but——

MARGOT. [*Translating* MARION's *" but " into her own idiom*] But that was the set-up. Well, he has been using that Nannie technique ever since. For twenty years he held you over Mary's head. And for the last eighteen months he has held Mary over mine.

MARION. Mary ! Is this true ? Mary, pay attention !

MARY. [*Dreamily*] I never noticed before what a nice face you have, Marion.

MARION. [*Sharply*] Mary ! Did John make me into a bogy for you ? I could never forgive him for that.

MARY. [*Kindly*] Not a bogy, exactly. Just a carrot.

MARION. A carrot ! Oh . . . [*light dawns*] Oh, I see what you mean about the donkey. Yes, of course. That is just what we have been. But to think that John . . . I can't believe it.

MARY. Do you mind if I ask you something, Marion ? It's something rather personal. Are you very good at arranging flowers ?

MARION. I loathe arranging flowers. A fiddling business. Why ?

MARY. Yes, I was afraid of that. Dear me, the hours I have wasted. I remember once throwing away some lovely herbaceous things and starting again on sweet-peas at the last moment, because they wouldn't come right.

MARION. You mean, because *I* was coming ?

MARY. I wouldn't be surprised if you're not even punctual. It was just John's way of getting his meals on time.

MARION. Is that how . . . [*words fail her*] The . . . [*she looks round for an appropriate epithet for her son, and at last finds one*] the *MONSTER !* You have no idea how much I tried to be a nice mother-in-law. Not coming too often, or interfering, or offering advice, or being last-generation about things. I was so pleased with myself, too! I prided myself on being a *model* mother-in-law. And all I've been is a bogy.

MARY. Not a bogy, Marion ; just a——

> *Before she can say " carrot ", the* WAITER *comes up with the wine.*

WAITER. The wine for madame.

MARGOT. Yes, that looks all right. Open it.

WAITER. Perhaps if it cooled a little longer . . .

MARGOT. No, we'll drink it now. Bring a third glass. Oh, you've brought one.

WAITER. I saw madame arrive.

MARY. Don't look so sad, Marion.

MARGOT. That isn't sorrow. It's helpless rage.

MARION. You are right, Margot. When I think of my wasted opportunities. The things I could have done.

MARGOT. With what ?

MARION. The back of a hair-brush.

MARGOT. Don't take it too hard, Marion. John's a genius in his way. To use the same technique on three generations and get away with it . . .

MARY. Two generations, Margot. Only Marion and I were fools. You saved the honour of womanhood.

MARION. Mary darling, I doubt very much whether you should have champagne. What are we going to drink to ? [*Exit* WAITER.]

MARGOT. To the damnation of John.

MARION. To our emancipation from John.

MARY. No ; no, we will drink to Margot.

MARION. To Margot ?

MARY. Because she belongs to a generation that will have no more Johns.

MARION. [*Laughing*] To you, Margot, with all my heart !

MARY. To Margot !

MARGOT. [*Heartily agreeing*] To me !

CURTAIN

CLARION CALL

CHARACTERS

In order of appearance

POLLY ANLISS.
MRS. WEBB.
MRS. ANLISS.

SAMMY WOOD.
TOMMY ANLISS.

The scene is the living-room of a lower middle-class family in a provincial town. At the back, left, is a window, and right of it the door opening on to the street. Left is the fireplace, decorated with overmantel. Down, left, the open door to the kitchen. The room is very neat and clean, and the furnishings what one would expect. By the right wall is a sofa; two easy-chairs by the fire, one basket and one, the veteran of more than one auction sale, of leather. In the middle is a table set for tea. There are flowers, and the china and the cloth are obviously the best; one is aware that this is an occasion.

When the curtain goes up a girl of eighteen or so is putting the finishing touches to the table, not with any air of anticipation, but with a gloomy suggestion of doing her duty. A middle-aged woman, MRS. ANLISS, the girl's mother, is preening herself at the mirror over the fireplace, and her friend, MRS. WEBB, who has obviously "run in", is standing on the opposite side of the table from the fire, admiring the spread. On the sofa sits SAMMY WOOD, a reporter; young, untidy, bored by the job. He is still wearing his overcoat, unbuttoned and spread voluminously round him, and is playing with his soft hat.

In sheer exuberance MRS. WEBB leans over and tweaks a flower into place in the vase. POLLY stops her own tweakings at once.

POLLY. [*Coldly*] Does it not please you, Mrs. Webb ?

MRS. WEBB. Oh, now, dearie, no offence meant. My mind wasn't thinking what my hand was doing. I'm that excited.

MRS. ANLISS. A quarter past already. Oh, my, but my heart

91

hasn't beaten like this since I had indigestion in the spring. Do I look all right?

WOOD. You look like a bride, Mrs. Anliss.

MRS. ANLISS. Well, let me tell you, Mr. Wood, I'm a deal more excited this minute than I was on my wedding day. Cool as a cucumber, I was, and everyone said so. It was John who was all of a dither. Always was excitable, John was. That's why I've been a widow this fifteen years, Mr. Wood. Just wore himself out dashing from one thing to another. The boy who's coming home now was just like him. Always wanted something but the thing he had.

WOOD. [*With a hint of prompting*] But he was a nice boy, Mrs. Anliss. You were very fond of him.

MRS. ANLISS. [*Matter of fact*] Of course I was fond of him. Wasn't he my only son?

MRS. WEBB. Ah, he was a nice boy, Tommy. [*To* WOOD] High-spirited, you know, but always with a cheery word for everyone. I mind once he gave our Willy his Saturday penny because Will had fallen and hurt himself over at Roberts' fence.

WOOD. [*Pulling out his notebook*] A very fine spirit, Mrs. Anliss.

MRS. ANLISS. I don't remember that. I wonder what made him do it?

POLLY. He saw Mr. Roberts watching, and Mr. Roberts gave him sixpence. He bought striped balls, and ate them all himself, and he was sick all over the clean sheets on Saturday night.

MRS. ANLISS. Oh, yes, I remember the sheets.

WOOD. Oh, come, Miss Anliss! you mustn't remember your brother's childish escapades against him.

POLLY. I'm not remembering anything. It was Mrs. Webb who brought that up.

WOOD. Well, now, Miss Polly—Polly Anliss. Anyone ever call you polyanthus?

POLLY. Oh, yes. They called me that my first day in the infants.

WOOD. [*Hastily*] What do *you* remember most distinctly about the brother you haven't seen for seven years?

POLLY. That he always took the only sugar cookie on the plate.

WOOD. Dear me ; I hope you have provided well to-day.

MRS. ANLISS. I'm thinking with that fine ham the *Clarion* sent us we won't get the length of cookies. I really don't know why the *Clarion* should bother about folks like us.

WOOD. But it is folks like you who are the backbone of this nation, Mrs. Anliss. You brought up a fine son, and we have had the pleasure of restoring him to you ; and we are naturally interested in his homecoming, and anxious to share in the rejoicings. Wouldn't you—er—wouldn't you like a few more of your neighbours in to share your happiness with you ?

MRS. ANLISS. Mrs. Webb here is the only neighbour we care to have, thank you. If it comes to that, the neighbours weren't all that fond of Tommy.

WOOD. [*With a glance out of the window*] Judging by all the people at the doors and windows, they seem to be taking a great interest in his home-coming.

MRS. ANLISS. It doesn't take much to interest them. Do you think he'll be by the train or the bus ?

WOOD. If I knew that, Mrs. Anliss, I shouldn't be here waiting. I should have met him and brought him to you personally on behalf of my paper.

MRS. WEBB. It's a fine paper the *Clarion*. My man says you can't sprain your finger nowadays without the *Clarion* gives you compensation. He says they've made breaking a leg a positive pleasure.

WOOD. [*Repeating a lesson*] We like to feel that our public is our responsibility. We believe that a colossal organisation like ours should be used in the service of our readers. Since we began our Lost Friends department we have been the means of uniting no less than four hundred and fifty-seven couples who had lost sight of each other in the rush of life. Mothers and sons [*he bows a little to* MRS. ANLISS *to acknowledge her part in the great achievement*], husbands and wives, old friends who had gone different ways. The *Clarion* called them together. It is a pleasant experience, Mrs. Anliss, to share in human joy. We newspaper men see so much of the tragic side of life.

MRS. WEBB. Yes, you must see some awful things. When young Mrs. Apfel committed suicide there was a reporter there before the police. Had a camera and all. Her husband threw him out of the window before he could get anything, though. A nice young man, he seemed. I was sorry for him. Quite worried over the camera being broken, he was. They cost quite a bit, it seems.

MRS. ANLISS. Are you going to take our photos?

WOOD. I am.

MRS. ANLISS. Dear me, fancy me being in the paper!

WOOD. Of course, I can't guarantee that it will appear. That depends on one of the editors. He decides what goes in, and it may be that in a pressure of news he chooses something else.

POLLY. The little boy who stuck his head through the railings and couldn't get it back; or the parrot and the kitten that eat together.

MRS. ANLISS. Polly Anliss, I don't know what is wrong with you. It ill becomes any member of this house——

The door is burst open by an excited woman, and a crowd of women and girls can be seen behind her.

[*Chorus*]. He's coming, Mrs. Anliss! He's coming! Here he is, coming up the street!

WOOD *darts out of the room, through the crowd at the door, and is seen passing the window. A moment later he reappears escorting a young man. The crowd at the door, who have turned to watch his advent, give back with little cries of "Well, well, here he is! Welcome back, Tommy!" WOOD leads in a youth of twenty-two whose bearing is a mixture of swagger and embarrassment.*

WOOD. Mrs. Anliss, I have great pleasure on behalf of the *Daily Clarion* in restoring your son to you.

There is a feeble cheer from the women who have crowded round the door again.

MRS. ANLISS. Well, Tommy.

TOMMY. Hullo, Ma.

WOOD. Aren't you going to kiss your mother, my boy?

TOMMY *kisses his mother.*

WOOD. And your sister. You haven't forgotten your sister in seven years, have you?

TOMMY. Is that Polly ? Help ! You were a kid last time I saw you. I suppose you don't remember me at all ?

POLLY. Oh, I remember you all right.

MRS. ANLISS. And you remember Mrs. Webb ?

TOMMY. Willy Webb's mother ? Oh, yes. How are you ? [*He shakes hands.*]

WOOD. Well, Mrs. Anliss, now for the photograph. Just here, I think. [*He manœuvres* MRS. ANLISS *and her son into the corner by the door so that the crowd make a background, several having been pushed forward so far in the excitement that they are now definitely in the room.* POLLY *slips out by the door, left, to the kitchen and thence outside.*] Come along, Mrs. Webb.

MRS. WEBB. Oh, but I'm not a relation, you know. I'm only a neighbour.

WOOD. You may not be a relation, but you are a registered reader. Just here, Mrs. Webb. That's right. [*To* TOMMY *and his mother*] I think it would be more appropriate if you embraced each other, don't you ?

TOMMY. [*Doubtfully*] Well, we were never much on hugging.

WOOD. Put your arm round her, then. [*He assists* TOMMY *to put a limp left arm on* MRS. ANLISS'S *shoulder.*] Now, Mrs. Anliss, you hold his hand so [*puts* MRS. ANLISS'S *right hand into the dangling right hand of her son, and bending both at the elbow, as if they were dolls*]. Now, Miss Polly. Why, where is Miss Polly ? [MRS. ANLISS *moves as if to go in search of her.*] No, don't move, Mrs. Anliss ! Keep just where you are. [*He goes to the door, left, which* POLLY *has shut behind her, opens it, and calls*] Miss Polly ! Miss Polly, we're taking the photograph ! Miss Polly !

TOMMY. Oh, never mind Polly. Let's get it over with.

WOOD. [*Coming back*] Well, all ready ? Don't jump when the light flares. Look happy everyone. This is a joyful occasion. [*The three principals stand in strained attitudes, while the intruding neighbours crane grinning behind. He takes the photograph.*]

MRS. WEBB. Oh ! I never could bear these things. Worse than the Fifth of November.

WOOD. There we are ! [*Bundling up*] Well, that's that ! [*The relief in his voice is more apparent than he knows, but no one is interested in him.*] Now I must leave you to your celebration.

MRS. ANLISS. Oh, but you're going to stay and have some of the ham with us, and a cup of tea, aren't you ?

WOOD. That's very nice of you, Mrs. Anliss, very nice. If my time were my own I should be delighted to. But I am merely the slave of the *Clarion*, you know. [*Hastily*] A happy slave, of course ; a Mercury. But a mere servant. My paper will be waiting to hear all about your son's arrival, and beyond the paper is the public. I must go, Mrs. Anliss. It has given me great pleasure to be present at your reunion. On behalf of the paper I congratulate you both, and hope that you will have long-continued happiness together. [*He shakes hands with MRS. ANLISS, TOMMY, and as an afterthought, with MRS. WEBB.*]

MRS. ANLISS. [*As she shakes hands*] I'm sure we're all very grateful.

WOOD. [*To the neighbours*] Now, good people, since both you and the *Daily Clarion* have seen Tommy safely home, I suggest that we all leave him in the arms of his family for a little quiet chat over old times. [*He shepherds the crowd expertly out of the doorway, and waves his hat to the family.*] Goodbye everyone.

MRS. ANLISS. Goodbye, Mr. Wood. Pleased to see you any time you're by. Just drop in.

WOOD. That's the idea, Mrs. Anliss. We're all friends on the paper.　　　　　　　[*Exit, and shuts door. Enter POLLY from the left.*

MRS. ANLISS. I don't know what all these people wanted to push in for. It would suit Mrs. Bell better to wash her front room curtains. [*Turning and seeing POLLY*] Where did you get to, Polly Anliss ? You must have heard Mr. Wood shouting for you !

POLLY. I heard him all right.

MRS. ANLISS. Then why couldn't you be polite enough to answer. I don't know what he must have thought.

TOMMY. Oh, never mind Polly. When are we going to have tea ?

MRS. ANLISS. Yes, yes. I'm forgetting. You must be hungry after that long journey. You know, I can hardly believe that you're Tommy. You've grown a lot since fifteen.

MRS. WEBB. A fine man he's grown into.

TOMMY. You haven't changed, Ma. You don't look a day older.

MRS. ANLISS. [*Pleased*] Are you starting telling fibs the minute you're inside the house ? Polly, is the kettle boiling ?

POLLY. Just about.

MRS. ANLISS. Well, make the tea, girl ; don't stand there. [*Exit* POLLY.] Sit down, Tommy, sit down. [*She indicates one of the easy-chairs, but* TOMMY *pulls out a chair from the table and sits in it.*]

TOMMY. And how's Willy, Mrs. Webb ? Still hanging round the old town ?

MRS. WEBB. [*Stung but controlled*] I don't know so much about hanging round. He has a good job with Parker's garridge. Three fifteen a week, and he's engaged to a fine girl and putting by every week for the wedding. No need for him to leave town. [*In spite of herself she cannot keep the emphasis off the pronoun.*]

MRS. ANLISS. Of course not. Willy's a good son to his mother, and he'll make a good husband to his girl. A son to be proud of.

TOMMY. [*Rising to the implication*] Meaning that I'm not.

MRS. ANLISS. Well, I don't exactly boast about you yet.

TOMMY. [*Smugly*] But you thought enough of me to advertise for me to come.

MRS. ANLISS. I couldn't help wondering where you'd got to.

TOMMY. Oh. Just curiosity.

MRS. ANLISS. I don't know about curiosity. The thought of you was always dig-digging at me when I had nothing else to do. I couldn't put my feet up for a minute but you'd come into my mind and spoil my rest. It was like having a tap dripping somewhere when you're warm in bed at nights. So when the *Clarion* started finding lost friends and that, I thought I'd just as well to give them your name. They don't charge anything.

TOMMY. And I suppose if they'd charged something you wouldn't have done it !

MRS. ANLISS. Well, they mightn't have found you. How was I to know ? If I'd been sure they'd find you, I would have paid up quite willing, for the peace of mind it gives me. It's nice to know your not in prison or anything.

TOMMY. In prison ! Well, I like that !

Mrs. Anliss. Well, how was I to know ? It's just as likely as making a fortune. [*Enter* Polly *with tea and hot water.*] Here's tea. Draw in your chair, Mrs. Webb.

Mrs. Anliss *sits with her back to the fire,* Polly *opposite her,* Tommy *facing the audience, and* Mrs. Webb *with her back to it.* Mrs. Anliss *pours tea.*

Mrs. Anliss. Polly, carve the ham. [Polly *begins to carve.*] Your hair's grown a lot darker, Tommy. Two lumps, Mrs. Webb. [*She sugars* Mrs. Webb's *tea.*] How many do you take now, Tommy ? Funny not knowing my own son's tastes, isn't it ?

Tommy. Three lumps, and another for luck. [*To* Polly] No fat for me.

Polly. It's all fat.

Tommy. Well, cut till you find some lean for me. What did you buy a ham that was all fat for ?

Mrs. Anliss. We didn't buy it. The *Daily Clarion* sent us it as a present.

Tommy. Oh, then of course it's all fat !

Mrs. Anliss. I don't think you need speak like that about the *Clarion*. It's thanks to the *Clarion* you're here. We should all be grateful to them.

Mrs. Webb. It was a nice thought, I think, sending the ham.

Tommy. Thought ! You don't imagine they thought about it, do you ? They bought hams wholesale from the docks at tuppence the pound, so they could sling one out to everyone they united.

Mrs. Webb. Why should they do a thing like that ?

Tommy. Why should they pay my fare home ? Just advertisement ! It's a wonder they haven't *Daily Clarion* printed on the ham.

Polly *unconsciously tilts the ham a little so that she can look underneath.*

Mrs. Anliss. Pay your fare ! Did they do that ?

Tommy. Of course they did ; I'm here, aren't I ? They stalled about it at first, but I said no fare nothing doing, so they forked out. It looks well in the account, see ? " Mr. Anliss, not being in affluent circs., etc., etc., the *Daily Clarion* came to the rescue, etc., etc."

Mrs. Anliss. And you're pleased to have that published about you! That you hadn't the money to come to see your folks after seven years.

Tommy. They can say anything they like about me as long as they give me three quid for nothing. They tried to palm me off with a railway ticket, but I said I couldn't go home in the clothes I was wearing. So they forked out.

Mrs. Anliss. Tommy Anliss, I'm ashamed of you, downright ashamed. Haven't you an atom of self-respect in your composition?

Tommy. Oh, don't start jawing the minute I'm in the house. Here I come from the other end of the country to see you and all you do is jaw.

Mrs. Anliss. You wouldn't have come at all, I don't wonder, if you didn't get your fare paid.

Tommy. Well, you didn't spend anything on advertising for me, did you? So we're quits.

Mrs. Webb. Did you find it hard to get leave off from your business? Most bosses are terrible mean with holidays.

Tommy. [*Airily*] Oh, no. I'm very much my own master. I take my holidays when I think I will.

Polly. What exactly is your business?

Tommy. I'm an agent.

Mrs. Anliss. For what?

Tommy. Anything that has an agency.

Mrs. Anliss. You're not a bookie, are you?

Polly. He'd have had the money to come home if he'd been a bookie.

Tommy. Who said I hadn't the money to come home! All I said was that I'd be a fool to spend money if the *Clarion* would spend it for me.

Mrs. Webb. [*Kindly*] There's nothing wrong with that, Tommy.

Tommy. [*To his mother*] Talking of money, I suppose you wouldn't like to put a little into my business?

Mrs. Anliss. [*Simply*] I wouldn't.

Tommy. Not even if I showed you a record of the commissions I made last year?

MRS. ANLISS. Not even if you took me in person to a gold mine and pulled chunks out of the ground to show me.

TOMMY. I was afraid you wouldn't. This family never had any enterprise. Always afraid to take a chance.

MRS. ANLISS. And when did you ever show any enterprise?

POLLY. Well, he did take Father's watch with him when he left.

TOMMY. Of course I did. Sons have first right to their fathers' watches. And what good was it doing wrapped up in cotton wool in a drawer?

MRS. ANLISS. If I didn't know that it was the only thing between you and certain starvation, I would have been much angrier about that watch than I was. Did you pawn it, or did you sell it?

TOMMY. Neither.

MRS. ANLISS. You didn't part with it! Why, Tommy——

TOMMY. I auctioned it.

MRS. ANLISS. Auctioned!

TOMMY. You can get far more out of two men wanting the same watch than out of one man that has to be persuaded he wants one at all.

MRS. WEBB. [*Genuine*] You're that cute, Tommy, it's a wonder to me you're not a millionaire.

TOMMY. I wonder myself sometimes.

POLLY. You have to work to be a millionaire.

TOMMY. What do you do, Polly? Just " put the kettle on " ?

MRS. ANLISS. Polly has a very good job with the bus company. In the office. She's in charge of her own department now.

TOMMY. And what do they give you for that?

POLLY. They don't give it to me. I earn it. And it keeps me and Mother very comfortably, thank you.

MRS. WEBB. Ay, they're a good firm, the buses. And getting bigger every day. They've made a big difference to this town, even if they are a mixed blessing.

TOMMY. Mixed? What's wrong with buses?

MRS. WEBB. [*Going on with her explanation even before he has asked*] In the old days I didn't have to see that sister-in-law of mine more than twice a year. We went to her when the goose-berries were ripe, and she came to us at Christmas. But now she's in and out of town as free as a wasp. I suppose you came by train, Tommy.

TOMMY. No, I came by road.

MRS. ANLISS. One of Gaffney's buses, was it ?

TOMMY. No, a lorry. A chap I know was coming north with a load. He gave me a lift.

POLLY. [*Into the pause*] Did you buy the postcard yourself ?

TOMMY. Card ?

POLLY. The postcard that said : Expect me Tuesday afternoon.

TOMMY. Smarty ! You'll never get a husband if you chip a fellow like that.

POLLY. What makes you think I want one ?

TOMMY. I don't *think*. Every girl wants a husband.

POLLY. That's just a male superstition. For your information [*that is an echo of " the Office "*] no girl *ever* wants a husband.

TOMMY. No ? Then why does she work so hard to get one !

POLLY. Because some other girl's got one. It would be the same if it was some kind of hat. It's the fashion, that's all. But it's not nearly so fashionable as it used to be.

MRS. ANLISS. [*Indulgently*] Polly, you talk an awful lot of nonsense.

POLLY. The first girl that found a whole week's wages in her hand on Friday night instead of what was left over after the pub and the " dogs " and the " pools ", she started a new fashion. A hundred years from now it'll be a disgrace to have a husband. They'll have to be hidden in back rooms out of sight ; like keeping pet rabbits in a tenement.

TOMMY. You know, if you're not careful you'll find yourself preaching off a soap-box at a street corner.

POLLY. What would I waste my time preaching to men about ?

TOMMY. Why men ?

POLLY. You don't find women standing round street corners. They're busy washing up, and mending the socks the men have stood through.

MRS. WEBB. [*Once more kindly bridging a social gulf*] I suppose you're not married, are you, Tommy ?

TOMMY. Not me! I'll look them over a while longer before I pick one.

POLLY. I hope you provide shelter for the queue.

TOMMY. [*To* MRS. WEBB] How's Liz?

MRS. WEBB. Oh, Liz is fine, thank you, fine. She——

TOMMY. [*Patronising*]. I'll maybe have time to drop round and see her after tea.

POLLY. I shouldn't, if I were you.

TOMMY. No? And why not, may I ask? Afraid the wicked prodigal will upset the little stay-at-home?

POLLY. Not exactly; but she's expecting her third any day now.

TOMMY. [*Flatly*] Oh? Married, is she?

MRS. ANLISS. Things haven't stood still since you left town, you know, Tommy.

TOMMY. [*Recovering*] I should say not! Three's going it a bit, isn't it?

MRS. ANLISS. They can afford it. Liz did well for herself. A car, and a maid, and stalls every Saturday at the Palladium.

MRS. WEBB. There's good money in the motor business these days. [*Tentatively*] You wouldn't be interested in that, would you, Tommy? Jim was saying there was a vacancy in the west garage. Good prospects, he said, if the——

TOMMY. What! Me settle down in this town?

MRS. ANLISS. What's wrong with the town? One town's very like another when you're settled. A Boots, an International, a Woolworths, and some baker or other; who's to tell whether they are in Plymouth or Paisley?

TOMMY. The football teams are different. Oh, I suppose the town's all right for a chap that's content with a weekly wage and a ten-shilling bonus at Christmas. But there's no scope in it.

MRS. ANLISS. Scope for what, may I ask?

TOMMY. For a fellow with ideas.

MRS. WEBB. [*Genuine*] Have you got ideas, Tommy?

TOMMY. Bursting with them. Take it from me, if you want to get anywhere you've got to have ideas.

POLLY. You haven't got an idea you're Napoleon, have you? That gets you into an asylum.

TOMMY. No ; and when I'm living in Park Lane, young Polly, I won't ask *you* to stay.

POLLY. No one lives in Park Lane any more. They live in Belgrave Square.

TOMMY. [*Stung*] How do you know ?

POLLY. Even a burglar knows that.

MRS. ANLISS. Well, I only hope that your ideas won't get you into trouble. It seems to me that half the police court cases in the *Clarion* start with someone getting notions. And a lot of good ideas go bad on folks. Like people inventing gunpowder and forgetting to get out of the way. And there's the law, you know.

TOMMY. I'm not proposing to be a criminal !

MRS. ANLISS. Perhaps not, but that's the catch. I read in the *Clarion* that there's practically nothing you can do but there's a law says you can't. They've just forgotten to reverse them. If they don't happen to like what you're doing, they look back to see what they can find, and sure enough you find yourself in jail. There's a law says you can be put to death for wearing red on Sunday, or something like that. So don't let them catch you with any ideas that they mightn't like.

TOMMY. Don't you worry, no one's catching me with anything.

MRS. WEBB. Perhaps when Tommy's had time to look round he'll like the old place so much he'll forget Park Lane. And I wouldn't wonder but—— [*There is a whistle outside*] Some-one whistling. [*As they pause to listen for its repetition*] Some of your old pals come to look you up, Tommy.

The whistle is repeated.

TOMMY. It's Harry ! [*He begins to eat the last few mouthfuls of his meal in haste.*]

MRS. ANLISS. Who's Harry ?

TOMMY. I didn't think he'd be so soon.

MRS. ANLISS. If he's a friend, you'd better bring him in for some tea.

TOMMY. He's not exactly a friend . . . [*At the window, peering sideways down the street*] Yes, it's Harry. [*With a wave of his arm to indicate acquiescence*] Coming ! He's the chap that gave me the lift. He just dropped some goods here, and then he's going east to Marbury before he goes south to-morrow. We'll spend the night in Marbury. [*He is reaching for his coat and hat which are hanging on the back of the door.*]

MRS. ANLISS. [*Staggered*] You mean you're going away with him? Now?

TOMMY. That's the idea.

MRS. ANLISS. But you've only just come home! What will Mr. Wood think!

TOMMY. [*Bending over to gulp the remains of his tea*] Who's Mr. Wood?

MRS. ANLISS. The gentleman from the *Clarion*.

TOMMY. Oh, him! You don't imagine you'll ever see him again, do you? By this time he doesn't even remember what part of town you live in. Cheer up, Ma. It's been a good party, and maybe we'll have our photos in the paper to-morrow. Who knows? For once I'll have to buy a *Clarion*.

MRS. ANLISS. [*Still speaking out of her daze*] Don't you buy it regular?

TOMMY. Me? I don't buy anything but *Midday Specials*.

MRS. ANLISS. Then how did you . . .

TOMMY. Oh, the ad. I saw the paper in a tea shop one day. What about a couple of quid to help me on the way, Ma?

MRS. ANLISS. A couple of . . .! You've got a nerve! With three pounds from the *Clarion* lying in your pocket this minute.

TOMMY. [*Cheerfully*] Make it ten bob, then. For old sake's sake. Think how nice——

MRS. ANLISS. Not one penny will you get from me, you impudent good-for-nothing. [*This is said matter-of-factly, and without any great feeling.*]

TOMMY. O.K., Ma, O.K. If you change your mind the Ritz will always find me. [*He pockets a couple of scones from the table, pats his mother on the back*] Let me know when Polly gets married so that I can come home and say I told you so! So long, Mrs. Webb. Say hullo to Willy for me!

> *He goes. The three women stare in silence at the door.*

POLLY. Well! I can sleep in my own bed after all.

MRS. WEBB. [*Whose soft heart is afraid that MRS. ANLISS may be hurt*] He's just thoughtless, Mrs. Anliss. He's young yet.

MRS. ANLISS. [*Still staring at the door*] And that's what I changed my wash day for !

MRS. WEBB. [*Preparing to go*] Well, it's time I popped back and put Bill's meat on the stove.

MRS. ANLISS. You'll do nothing of the sort. It's not near that time yet, and you know it. You just wait till I get out of these corsets, and we'll have some fresh tea in peace and comfort. Polly, see to the kettle, and put away that lump of lard [*she is referring to the* Clarion *ham*]. And give the fire a bit stick. It's near out with all the excitement. You'll find yesterday's *Clarion* under the cushion. [*She makes for the door, left.*

POLLY *picks the* Clarion *from under the chair cushion.*

MRS. WEBB. [*Anxious to express her goodwill*] Would you like me just to give these cups a swill ?

POLLY. [*All sweetness and light*] Thank you, Mrs. Webb. That would be very kind of you. [*As* MRS. WEBB *begins to gather the cups together ; pausing in the act of tearing the page, and reading*] " Miss Margaret Rains and her only brother, who, having been parted for twenty years, were united yesterday by the kind offices of the *Clarion*." I wonder if they found any lean in their ham ?

She tears with a will as the curtain comes down.

CURTAIN

REMEMBER CÆSAR

CHARACTERS

In order of appearance

LORD WESTON.
ROGER CHETWYND.
LADY WESTON.

A room in the house of RICHARD, LORD WESTON, *on a spring morning in the reign of Charles II.* LORD WESTON (*until his late elevation to the bench, Sir Richard*) *is not wealthy, and the room is a combination of study and withdrawing-room. Up right is the door to the landing (it is a first-floor room), in the rear wall a large casement window looking out to the front of the house, in the left wall the fireplace and, down, another window through which one can see the trees in the garden. Up from the fireplace a cupboard in the wall. Hanging on the walls and over the fireplace are family portraits.*

LORD WESTON *is seated by the fireplace, a table of books and papers beside him. He is engaged in filling his pipe. And talking.*

Down right, where the light from the side window falls across his small writing-table, is seated MR. ROGER CHETWYND, *a thin, earnest, absent-minded, and conscientious youth. So conscientious is he that his mind, even when absent, is absent on his employer's business. He has begun by listening to his master's lecture, but the lure of his work has been gradually too much for him, and he is now blissfully copying from one paper on to another while the measured words flow over him, his lips forming the phrases while he writes.*

WESTON. —And furthermore [*he pauses to arrange the tobacco*] it is not alone a question of duty ; there is your own success in the world to be considered. It is not your intention to be a secretary all your life, is it ? No. Very well. Diligence, and a respect for detail should be your care. I did not become Lord

106

Weston by twiddling my thumbs and hoping for favours. I won my honours by hard work and zealous service. Men who were at Corpus Christi with me are to-day copying documents for a living, while I—let us not mince matters—am the best-known, and certainly the most impartial, judge in England, and a favoured servant of his gracious majesty, Charles the Second. That, I submit, my good Roger, is an example to be studied. It is not only unbecoming in you to ask for a half-holiday, but it is greatly unlike you. I fear . . . [*He has turned towards his secretary, and discovers his misplaced diligence. After a pause, coldly*] Can it be, Mr. Chetwynd, that you have not been listening to my discourse ?

ROGER. [*Brought to the surface by the cessation of the word music*] What, my lord ? Oh, no. Yes, certainly, sir, I am listening.

WESTON. What was I talking of ?

ROGER. Yourself, sir. [*Amending*] I mean, of your rise to success, my lord. [*It is apparent that it is an oft-heard tale.*]

WESTON. We were talking of your extraordinary request for a half-holiday, when you had one only last month. On that occasion, if I remember well, your parents came to town and you must needs go gadding. Would it be straining courtesy too far if I were to enquire what prompts this new demand for heedless leisure ?

ROGER. I thought perhaps if you did not need me this afternoon, my lord, I might personally interview the clerk of the Awards Committee, and find out why he has not sent that document.

WESTON. [*A little taken aback*] Oh. Oh, indeed.

ROGER. The lack of it greatly hinders. It holds up my work, you see. And at this most interesting point . . . [*His glance goes longingly to his desk.*]

WESTON. That, of course, is a different matter. I see no reason [*he looks for a spill for his pipe, first on the table and then, rising, by the fire*] why you should not take a walk to Mr. Clay's in the afternoon if the weather is fine. I am relieved that your thoughts are on sober matters, as befits a rising young man. Diligence, courage, and attention to detail : these are the three

. . . Where are the spills ? These are what bring a man to success and endow him with dignity . . . No tapers and no spills, as usual ! [*Looking on the table for a scrap of paper and finally feeling in his pockets*] Without an orderly mind no man can hope [ROGER *has gone back to his work*] to excel in any of the learned professions. [*He has found a scrap of paper, rather crushed, in his pocket and smooths it out, uninterestedly, to make a rough spill.*] Detail, my good Roger, attention to detail. That is the beginning of greatness. That is the . . . [*reading automatically and with some difficulty what is written on the scrap of paper*] " Remember Cæsar." [*Repeating, with vague interest*] " Remember Cæsar." [*He turns the paper back and forth, at a loss. And then a new idea occurs to him, a rather horrible idea. To* ROGER] What is the date to-day ? [*As* ROGER, *buried again in his work, does not answer*] Roger ! I said, what day of the month is it ?

ROGER. [*Hardly pausing*] It is the fourteenth, my lord.

WESTON. The fourteenth ! The fourteenth of March. The Ides of March ! [*Looking at the paper again ; in a horrified whisper*] " Remember Cæsar " ! [*Louder*] So they want to kill me, do they ? They want to kill me ? [ROGER *comes to the surface, surprised.*] That is what it is to be a judge over men [*all his pompousness is dissolving in agitation*], an instrument of justice. Sooner or later revenge lies await in the by-ways. And the juster a judge has been, the more fearless [*he waves the paper in the astonished* ROGER'S *face*], so much greater will be the hate that pursues——

ROGER. What is it, my lord ? What is it ?

WESTON. My death warrant if I am not careful. What cases have we had lately ? The treason affair—I refused to be bribed ! [*The boast gives him a passing comfort.*] The piracy—both sides hate me for that ! Or there was that footpad——

ROGER. Is it a threat, the paper ? Where did it come from ?

WESTON. It was in my pocket. Someone must have . . . Yes, now I remember. A man brushed against me yesterday as I was leaving the courts. A small, evil-looking fellow, very sly.

ROGER. What does it say, the paper ?

WESTON. [*Much too occupied with his own fate to attend to his secretary's curiosity*] Just at the door, it was, and he didn't wait

LADY WESTON. I'm not. But the surest way to make me is to pat my hand and tell me not to be.

WESTON. My dear, your husband's life is in grave danger.

LADY WESTON. The last time it was in danger you had been eating game pie. What is it this time?

WESTON. [*Annihilating her flippancy with one broadside*] Assassination!

LADY WESTON. Well, well! You always wanted to be a great man and now you have got your wish!

WESTON. What do you mean?

LADY WESTON. They don't assassinate nobodies.

WESTON. [*Showing her the paper*] Read that, and see if you can laugh.

LADY WESTON. I'm not laughing. [*Trying to read the writing*] What a dreadful scrawl.

WESTON. Yes, the venomous scribbling of an illiterate.

LADY WESTON. [*Deciphering*] "Remember Cæsar." Is it a riddle?

WESTON. It is a death warrant. Do you know what day this is?

LADY WESTON. Thursday.

WESTON. What day of the month.

LADY WESTON. About the twelfth, I should guess.

WESTON. [*With meaning*] It is the fourteenth. The fourteenth of March.

LADY WESTON. Lawdamussy! Your good-sister's birthday! And we haven't sent her as much as a lily!

WESTON. I have deplored before, Frances, the incurable lightness of your mind. On the fourteenth of March Cæsar was murdered in the Forum.

LADY WESTON. Yes, of course. I remember. They couldn't stand his airs any longer.

WESTON. [*Reproving*] He was a great man.

LADY WESTON. [*Kindly*] Yes, my dear, I am sure he was. [*Looking again at the scrap of paper*] And is someone thinking of murdering you?

WESTON. Obviously.

LADY WESTON. I wonder someone hasn't done it long ago.

[*Before the look of wonder can grow in his eye*] A great many people must hate judges. And you are a strict judge, they say.

WESTON. It is the law that is strict. I am a judge, my good Frances, not a juggler. I have never twisted the law to please the mob, and I shall not please them by dying on the day of their choice.

LADY WESTON. No, of course not. You shall not go out of the house to-day. A nice light dinner and a good glass of——

WESTON. I have sent Roger to barricade all the doors, and I think it would be wise to close the ground-floor shutters and see that they are not opened for any——

LADY WESTON. Is it the French and the Dutch together you are expecting! And this is the morning Mr. Gammon's boy comes with the groceries. How am I to——

WESTON. My dear, is a little pepper more to you than your husband's life ?

LADY WESTON. It isn't a little pepper, it's a great deal of flour. And you would be the first to complain if the bread were short, or the gravy thin. [*Giving him back the paper*] How do you know that the little paper was meant for you ?

WESTON. Because it was in my pocket. I found it there when I was looking for something to light my pipe. [*With meaning*] There were no spills.

LADY WESTON. No spills. What, again ? Richard, you smoke far too much.

WESTON. [*Continuing hastily*] It was slipped into my pocket by a man who brushed against me yesterday. A dark, lean fellow with an evil face.

LADY WESTON. I don't think he was very evil.

WESTON. What do you know about it ?

LADY WESTON. It was kind of him to warn you. And wasn't it a mercy that the spills were finished and that no one had made any more ! If there had been even one there you would never have seen the paper. You would have gone for your noon walk down the Strand and someone would have stuck you like a goose on a spit, and I should have been a widow before dinner-time——

WESTON. [*Sinking into a chair*] Stop, Frances, stop ! It upsets me to——

    Enter ROGER, *a little out of breath after his flying tour round the house.*

WESTON. Ah, Roger. Have you seen to it all ? Every door barred, every window shut, all workmen out——

ROGER. [*A little embarrassed*] Every door except the kitchen one, my lord.

WESTON. [*Angry*] And why not the kitchen one ?

ROGER. [*Stammering*] The cook seemed to think . . . That is, she said . . .

WESTON. Well, speak, man, what did she say, and how does what the cook thinks affect my order to bar the kitchen door ?

ROGER. [*In a rush*] The cook said she was a respectable woman and had never been behind bars in her life and she wasn't going to begin at her age, and she was quite capable of dealing with anyone who came to the kitchen door——

LADY WESTON. Never mind, Roger, I shall speak to cook——

WESTON. [*Interrupting her, furious*] Is the woman mad ? Did you tell her that her master might be killed in her very presence if the door were not——

ROGER. I did, my lord, I did. She said there would be a killing there and then if I did not leave her kitchen. She is a very formidable woman, my lord, and there was the matter of a rolling-pin . . . I thought it best to desist.

LADY WESTON. Be calm, Richard. It is only that the cook's temper is apt to be uncertain in the morning. I know how to coax her into a better humour——

WESTON. Coax ! Since when have my servants to be coaxed ! She shall leave my house this very hour.

LADY WESTON. Oh, nonsense, Richard ! All cooks are strange tempered. It comes from standing over hot stoves and breathing in pepper. I shall see——

WESTON. This very hour ! If her silly mind is so careless of her master's safety she has no right to his roof. Tell her to pack her things and leave the house at once, and see that the door is barred after her.

LADY WESTON. And who will cook your pet dishes when I go to stay with Sibylla ? Be calm, Richard. The kitchen door will be locked, and cook will see to the barring of it herself, and be proud of her handiwork, I promise you. That is what a mistress is for, to sweep up after the master. I shall also see that all the downstairs windows are shuttered as you suggest. We can always haul the groceries through an upper window. That will be entertaining for poor old Lady Gascoigne, anyhow ; glooming there in her window. She has had no amusement out of this street since the dog-fight on Ash Wednesday. [*As she is going, pausing*] Would you like me to block up the chimneys, perhaps ?

WESTON. [*Controlling himself*] I think that so frivolous a suggestion at so anxious a time is in poor taste, Frances, and unworthy of you——

LADY WESTON. Did it appear frivolous to you ? How strange ! I had thought it odd to shutter the walls and yet leave openings in the roof that one could drive a coach and horses through. However ! [*She comes back into the room, takes two candelabra from different places in the room, and goes to the door.*]

WESTON. What do you want with these ?

LADY WESTON. If we are to·be in darkness below we shall want all the candles we can gather. [*Exit*

WESTON. The aptness of the female mind to busy itself about irrelevant and inconsiderable minutiæ is a source of endless wonder to me. [*Almost without noticing what he is doing he moves over to the fireplace and sticks his head into the chimney to view the width of it. As he withdraws it, he becomes aware of* ROGER, *standing watching.*] I see no reason now why you should not resume your work, Roger.

ROGER. Oh, my lord, it is beyond my power to work while you are in danger. Is there not something I could do ?

WESTON. [*Mightily flattered*] Nonsense, my good Roger, nonsense ! Nothing is going to happen to me.

ROGER. I could perhaps go and warn the authorities, and so prevent——

WESTON. [*Very brave*] No, no, no. Am I to spend the rest of

my life with a guard at my heels ?   A pretty figure I should cut !
Go on with your work and . . . [*his eye has lighted on a package
which is lying on a chair against the right wall.   The box is oblong
—roughly 18 in. by 10 in. by 4 in.—and tied with cord.   Sharply*]
What is this ?

ROGER.   That came for you this morning, sir.

WESTON.   What is it ?

ROGER.   [*With the faint beginnings of doubt in his voice*] I don't
know, my lord.   A man came with it and said that it was important that you should have it to-day.

WESTON.   And you didn't ask what it was !   You fool !

ROGER.   [*Humbly*] It didn't seem to be my business.   I never
do ask about the contents of your lordship's . . . I showed your
lordship the package when it came, and you said to leave it
there.

WESTON.   [*Peering with growing uneasiness at the thing*] The
man who brought it, what did he look like ?   Was he small ?
Dark ?

ROGER.   [*Who obviously had taken no notice*] I think he was
smallish.   But as to dark—his hat was pulled over his face.   I
think—I think he appeared to have a mole on his chin, but I
would not . . . It may have been just a——

WESTON.   A mole ?   [*His imagination at work*] A mole !   Yes.
Yes.   That man had a mole.   The man who brushed against me.
On the right side of his jaw.   I can see it as if he were standing
here.   We must get rid of this.   At once.

ROGER.   Do you think it is some infernal machine, sir ?   What
shall we do with it ?

WESTON.   [*Indicating the side window*] Open the window and
I shall throw it as far into the garden as I can.

ROGER.   But it may explode, sir, if we throw it.

WESTON.   What is certain is that it will explode if we do not !
How long has it been lying here ?

ROGER.   It came about nine o'clock, my lord.

WESTON.   [*In an agony*] Nearly three hours ago !   Open the
window, Roger.

ROGER.   No, sir.   You open the window.   Let me handle the
thing.   My life is nothing.   Yours is of great value to England.

WESTON. No, Roger, no. You are young. I have had my life. There are still great things for you to do in the world. You must live, and write my life for posterity. Do as I say. I promise you I shall exercise the greatest care. [*As* ROGER *rushes to the window*] No. Wait! A better idea. The gardener's pail. It is still on the landing!

ROGER. Yes! Yes, of course! [*He is out of the room and back in a moment with the wooden pail of water, which still has the wet cleaning rag hung over its edge.*]

WESTON. Stand back. [*He picks up the parcel gingerly.*] We do not know what satanic thing may happen. [*He inserts the parcel lengthwise into the pail, at full stretch of his arm, his head averted, his eyes watching from their extreme corners*] There is not enough water! Not enough to cover it.

ROGER. I'll get some. I shall not be a moment.

WESTON. No. Don't go. The flowers! [*He indicates a bowl of daffodils.*]

ROGER. Of course! [*He pulls the daffodils from their setting, throwing them on the desk in his agitation, and pours the water into the pail.*] Ah! That has done it!

WESTON. [*Dismayed, as he takes his hand from the package*] Now it is going to float! It must be wet through, or it is no use.

ROGER. We must put something heavy on top, to keep it down.

WESTON. Yes, yes. Get something.

ROGER. What shall I get?

WESTON. Good God, boy! Have you no ideas once the pen is out of your hand? Anything, anything that is heavy and that will fit into the pail. Books, anything!

ROGER. [*To whom books are objects of reverence, if not awe*] Books, sir? But they'll get very wet, won't they?

WESTON. In the name of heaven bring the first six books off the shelf!

ROGER. [*Snatching the books and bringing them*] I suppose it cannot be helped. Such beautiful bindings too! [*He picks the wet cloth off the edge of the pail, dropping it on the carpet, and plunges the books into the water, which very naturally overflows at this new incursion.*]

115

WESTON. [*Letting go his hold on the package and sitting back on his heels with a sigh of relief*] Ah! Well and truly drowned. [*He mops his forehead and* ROGER *collapses into the nearest chair.*]

>*Enter* LADY WESTON, *with a tray on which is a glass of wine and some biscuits.*

LADY WESTON. [*Seeing their strange occupation*] Lawdamussy, Richard! What have you got in the pail?

WESTON. A package that came this morning. The man who brought it was the same fellow that knocked against me yesterday and slipped that paper into my pocket. They thought I would open it, the fools! [*He is beginning to feel better.*] But we have been one too many for them!

LADY WESTON. [*In wild dismay*] But how stupid! You are just making a mess of the beautiful, brand-new——

WESTON. [*Interrupting her angrily*] Frances! [*The thunder of her name quenches her speech.*] What does your "beautiful brand-new" carpet matter when your husband's life is at stake? You shock me.

LADY WESTON. [*Who has not been going to say "carpet"*] Carpet? [*After a pause, mildly*] No, of course not, my dear. I should never dream of weighing your safety against even the finest product of Asia. Come and sit down and have a glass of wine. [*She puts the tray on his desk, gathering up the scattered daffodils as she does so*] You know how the doctor disapproves of excitement for you.

WESTON. Perhaps the doctor has never had an infernal machine handed in at his door of a spring morning.

>LADY WESTON *picks up the cloth from the floor, mops the spilt water, and pauses to look curiously at the contents of the pail as they catch her eye.*

ROGER. [*Who has been staring at the pail in absorbed fascination*] I am afraid we have made a little mess. Please let me do that.

LADY WESTON. [*In mild conversational tones*] That looks like Mr. Spencer in the water.

ROGER. Yes, it is. The thing floated, you see. And time was all-important. So it was imperative to take whatever was nearest to weight it down.

LADY WESTON. I see. [*Handing him the wet cloth, and the*

flowers] Would you be kind enough to take these downstairs ? [*She adds the empty flower-bowl to his load*] One of the maids will fill that for you. [ROGER *goes.*

WESTON. Have the kitchen wenches decided that the door of their domain may at last be bolted ?

LADY WESTON. Oh, they are all very happy. Cook thinks she knows how to make bullets by dropping hot lead into cold water, or something of the sort. And the kitchenmaid thinks that she will stay in London after all.

WESTON. Stay in London ?

LADY WESTON. [*Indicating his tray ; he is already sipping the wine*] Try the biscuits. They are Sibylla's recipe. Yes, she was leaving because she found London so quiet after the country.

WESTON. [*Through his biscuit*] Ridiculous !

LADY WESTON. In the country, she said, if there wasn't a calving there was a wedding, and if there wasn't a wedding there was a wake. It was never dull. A pleasant girl. I am glad London is being livelier for her.

WESTON. My household seem to treat my danger as a sort of raree-show.

LADY WESTON. No, dear, no. All maids like a little to-do. It makes life important for them.

WESTON. A little to-do ! My funeral, I hope will be even more exciting for them. You must have a wake to please the kitchen-maid.

LADY WESTON. [*Not listening to him ; contemplative, her eyes on the portrait which hangs opposite the side window*] Do you think we had better remove Great-aunt Cicely ?

WESTON. In the name of heaven, why ?

LADY WESTON. She is in the direct line of shots coming through that window.

WESTON. And why should any shots come through the window, may I ask ?

LADY WESTON. [*Mildly objecting to the tone*] I was merely taking thought for your property, my dear Richard. And anyone sitting in the ilex tree out there would be in a——

WESTON. [*On his feet*] Frances ! What made you think of the ilex tree ?

LADY WESTON. That is where I would shoot you from. I mean, if I were going to shoot you. The leaves are thick enough to hide anyone sitting there, and yet not enough to obscure their view.

WESTON. Come away from that window.

LADY WESTON. What?

WESTON. Come away from that window!

LADY WESTON. [*Moving to him*] No one is going to shoot *me*.

WESTON. [*Running out of the room, and calling to* ROGER *from the landing*] Roger! Roger!

ROGER. [*Very distant*] My lord?

WESTON. Has the gardener gone away yet?

ROGER. No, my lord. He is eating his dinner outside the kitchen window.

WESTON. Tell him to sit under the ilex tree until I give him leave to move.

ROGER. The ilex tree? Yes, my lord.

> WESTON *comes back and goes to the drawer of the table where his pistol is kept.*

LADY WESTON. [*As he takes out the pistol*] Oh, Richard, dear, be careful. That is a very dangerous weapon.

WESTON. [*Grimly important*] I know it!

LADY WESTON. It is so rusty that it is liable to do anything. [*As her husband proceeds to load the weapon*] You know that you haven't used it since you were shooting dancing balls off the fountain. That was the year after we were married. The butcher's son blew half his scalp off the other week, trying to fire a rusty pistol. He has no hair left except a few red tufts over the right ear. His father says the only hope for him is to become a gentleman so that he can wear a wig.

WESTON. There is nothing wrong with my pistol but a little dust.

LADY WESTON. Well, I think it is a poor way to foil an assassin.

WESTON. What is?

LADY WESTON. Blowing oneself up.

> *Enter* ROGER *with the bowl of daffodils.*

WESTON. [*Looking round at him as he comes in*] Has Joel gone to sit under the tree?

ROGER. Yes, sir. [*Putting down the bowl and making for the side window*] At least, I gave him your message.

WESTON. Keep away from that window! [*As* ROGER *looks astonished*] There may be someone in the ilex tree.

ROGER. But do you think they would try to shoot you as well as—as . . . [*he indicates the bucket*].

WESTON. Who knows? When you have dealt with the criminal mind as long as I have . . . Did you open the door to speak to the gardener?

ROGER. Oh, no, my lord. I spoke through the shutter. The cook is of the opinion that we should send for the military.

LADY WESTON. Cook is always of opinion that we should send for the military.

WESTON. [*Snapping the lock of his pistol*] Now we shall see whether there is anyone lurking in the tree. [*He moves over to the side of the window, peering out with the fraction of an eye.*]

LADY WESTON. Richard, if you are going to shoot off that thing, you will please wait until I——

> *She is interrupted by a loud knocking on the front door downstairs. This is such an unexpected development that all three are momentarily quite still, at a loss.* ROGER *is the first to recover.*

ROGER. Someone at the front door.

> *He moves over to the window in the rear wall, from which one can see the street. He is about to open the casement so that he may lean out to inspect the knocker, when* LORD WESTON *stops him.*

WESTON. [*Still at the fireplace*] Don't open that window!

ROGER. But I cannot see otherwise, my lord, who it is.

WESTON. If you put your head out of that window they may shoot without waiting to ask questions.

LADY WESTON. But, Richard, it may be some perfectly innocent visitor. [*The knocking is repeated.*

ROGER. If I were to stand on a chair . . . [*He brings a chair to the window and stands on it, but he is still not high enough to look down on whoever waits at the front door.*]

WESTON. Well? Well? Can you tell who it is?

ROGER. I am still not high enough, my lord.

119

LADY WESTON. Add the footstool, Roger.

> ROGER *adds the footstool to the chair, and aided by* LADY
> WESTON *climbs on to the precarious erection.*

LADY WESTON. Now, can you see anyone ?

ROGER. [*Having seen, scrambling down*] All is well, my lord. [*He throws open the casement, and calls to someone below*] In a moment, my good sir, in a moment ! All is well, my lord. It is only Mr. Cæsar. [*As this information is succeeded by a blank pause*] Shall I let him in ?

WESTON. Who did you say ?

ROGER. Mr. Cæsar. You remember : the man you met on Tuesday at Hampton, my lord. He was to come to see you this morning about rose trees. You made a note of it.

WESTON. [*Taking the crumpled piece of paper from his pocket in a dazed way*] I made a note ? " Remember Cæsar." Is that my writing ? Yes, it must be. Dear me !

LADY WESTON. You had better go down and let Mr. Cæsar in, Roger. Put the pistol away, Richard, dear ; your visitor might misunderstand it. [*She speaks cheerfully, as to a child ; it is obvious from her lack of surprise that excursions and alarms created by her husband over trifles are a normal part of existence for her.*] And if you take Mr. Spencer out of the water, I shall send Joel to take away the bucket. Perhaps Mr. Brutus would like some cordial ?

WESTON. Mr. *Cæsar.* [*He moves towards the bucket.*]

LADY WESTON. Of course. How could anyone forget a name like that ? And now, if you'll forgive me . . . It's my busy morning.

WESTON. [*Arresting her as she is going out of the door*] Oh, Frances ! What was in the parcel, do you think ?

LADY WESTON. That was your new velvet cloak, dear. I did try to tell you, you know. [*Exit.*

> *The curtain comes down on* LORD WESTON *ruefully taking
> the first dripping book from the water.*

CURTAIN